Cultural Globalization

A User's Guide

J. Macgregor Wise

Blackwell
Publishing

BLACKWELL PUBLISHING
350 Main Street, Malden, MA 02148-5020, USA
9600 Garsington Road, Oxford OX4 2DQ, UK
550 Swanston Street, Carlton, Victoria 3053, Australia

The right of J. Macgregor Wise to be identified as the author of this work has been asserted in accordance with the UK Copyright, Designs, and Patents Act 1988.

Designations used by companies to distinguish their products are often claimed as trademarks. All brand names and product names used in this book are trade names, service marks, trademarks, or registered trademarks of their respective owners. The publisher is not associated with any product or vendor mentioned in this book.

This publication is designed to provide accurate and authoritative information in regard to the subject matter covered. It is sold on the understanding that the publisher is not engaged in rendering professional services. If professional advice or other expert assistance is required, the services of a competent professional should be sought.

First published 2008 by Blackwell Publishing Ltd

2   2009

Library of Congress Cataloging-in-Publication Data

ISBN-13: 9780631235385 (hardback)
ISBN-13: 9780631235392 (paperback)

A catalogue record for this title is available from the British Library.

Set in 10.5/13pt Minion by Graphicraft Limited, Hong Kong.

The publisher's policy is to use permanent paper from mills that operate a sustainable forestry policy, and which has been manufactured from pulp processed using acid-free and elementary chlorine-free practices. Furthermore, the publisher ensures that the text paper and cover board used have met acceptable environmental accreditation standards.

For further information on
Blackwell Publishing, please visit our website at
www.blackwellpublishing.com

Contents

Preface		vii
Acknowledgments		ix
1	Culture at Home	1
	Culture	3
	Territory	10
	Identity	11
	Home	18
	Ideology and Hegemony	22
2	Culture and the Global	26
	Non-Local Connections	26
	Globalization	28
	Global Flows	34
	Form and Content, Local and Global	42
3	Global Youth	54
	Youth as a Contested Category	54
	Constructing Youth	55
	Surveillance and Youth	57
	Global Youth	62
	Core and Periphery	71
4	Global Music	76
	World Music and Cultural Imperialism	79

Contents

Global Flows of Music 86

Forms of Global Music 91

5 Territories of Cultural Globalization 108

Faye Wong 109

Dick Lee 111

Panlatinidad 118

Audiotopias 124

Citizenship 135

Conclusion: Opening Windows 148

References 155

Index 168

Preface

This book has as its subtitle *A User's Guide* since we are all, in one way or another, involved in cultural globalization and are *users* of global culture. It's a user's *guide*, but not a guidebook in any simple sense. It doesn't tell you what to do or where to go. The primary focus of the book is defined in the phrase *culture and identity*. This is not about economic, political, or even technological globalization. And it's not even about global culture *en toto*. I'm using examples of global youth culture and global music as a way to discuss the opening theory of culture, identity, and territory, but this is not an exhaustive examination, introduction, or critique of either global youth culture or global music. Most of my examples, though not all, are from Asian popular culture, but we'll range further afield as well. Throughout this book (as I will reiterate a few times in the pages to come), I consider the examples as *illustrative* but not necessarily representative (of youth culture, or music, more generally).

What follows is an *essay*, a specific form of writing. It is more personal and partial than other academic books. It is at times impressionistic, overly general, and overly specific. As such it may not be as theoretically satisfying to those seeking new theories of globalization, or as empirically satisfying to those who relish extensive ethnographic fieldwork. In many ways the essay itself follows the form of the home-making territorialization that is at the heart of the book. The essay is an assemblage of ideas, examples, questions, and strategies that I have collected over the past few years of thinking about issues of culture and globalization and everyday life. This is not a work of fieldwork, ethnography, or interviews. Rather I have pieced together a mosaic of bits which, it seems to me, fit into a larger picture. In other words, this assemblage works for me in that it helps me think through issues both theoretical and practical. It's a way of framing and responding to what I read in the newspaper, what I read in books, and what I gain from my interactions with people throughout my everyday life. Some of the pieces that make up this mosaic or assemblage are reproduced relatively faithfully, others have been wrenched out of their original contexts, reworked, and plunked back down in situations for which they were never meant. This is an essay that is not about being faithful to conceptual sources, but of taking concepts and seeing what they can do; letting them loose and watching them transform. To those who find their work in here, perhaps transformed, I mean no disrespect and hope that you see the creative potential of what I'm trying to do. This essay is not meant to encourage anyone to think only in this particular way, but to use what I have here as a means of beginning to think about one's own specificity, to ask one's own questions, and to search for one's own answers. My editor considers this book a work of ethics; I consider it a rant about connecting theory to everyday life. Perhaps they are the same thing.

Raymond Williams (1996, p. 177) once wrote of cultural studies that its purpose should be to take:

> the best we can in intellectual work and going with it in this very open way to confront people for whom it is not a way of life, for whom it is not in any probability a job, but for whom it is a matter of their own intellectual interest, their own understanding of the pressures on them, pressures of every kind, from the most personal to the most broadly political.

His admonition is the impetus behind this essay.

Acknowledgments

This book arose from teaching a number of classes at Clemson University and Arizona State University on global media and culture over the past decade or more. I want to thank all my students (but especially Esther Barraza) who, through their own working through of the material, their puzzled stares, and rich enthusiasms, contributed to the shaping of my own thoughts.

In acknowledging debts, I must mention Jayne Fargnoli, my editor at Blackwell. Thanks to you, Jayne, for your excitement at the initial proposal (donkey's years ago) and your support and infinite patience as this manuscript crept along. My thanks to Larry Grossberg, who gave me my foundation in cultural studies, my introduction to cultural theory and globalization, and who remains a cherished mentor and friend. My thanks to John Erni, Anthony Fung, Keehyeung Lee, and Raka Shome for all their insight and encouragement, and also to See Kam Tan (who tracked down some hard to find Dick Lee recordings for me) and Tony Mitchell (for additional resources on Dick Lee). Thanks to the anonymous reviewers at Blackwell who provided detailed and productive critiques of the draft of this book (they tried their best to mend my ways, the failures of this book are all mine). My thanks also to Caffe Java, The Coffee Plantation, The Coffee Bean and Tea Leaf, and, yes, Starbucks, for all the air conditioning and caffeine. My thanks to my parents for a truly unique upbringing, and to them, my sister, and extended family for all their support. And finally, my love and thanks to Elise, Catherine, and Brennen for being my touchstones.

1

Culture at Home

There is a story that I have heard enough times in the context of casual conversations with students here in Arizona to realize that it is not that uncommon. It is the story the speaker tells of being born in Mexico and moving to the United States with one's family at a young age. It is the story of returning to Mexico to visit relatives and being considered "too American" and living in the US and being considered "too Mexican." It is a story of negotiating between the cultures of home with one's parents and school with one's peers and work with one's colleagues. And all the while there is a realization that all these constituencies are pressing for one to make a choice: Which do you want to be? And one can't put off that choice forever. But there's also the feeling that there isn't much choice; these others have already made up their mind about what you are (or should be).

There is another story that I've been told, and that is a story where society presumes that the speaker fits the above story. That is, the speaker is frustrated that others keep assuming that just because one looks Latino that one must be a recent immigrant (legal or not) and that one must have a "real home" elsewhere or that one must be fraught with an identity crisis. And all this based on name and skin tone.

Sunaina Marr Maira (2002) tells a story of children of immigrants from India living in the US who, when they go off to college, become more "Indian" than they had been growing up. They profess a passion for traditional Indian customs, music, dance, film, and food, begin to hang out almost exclusively with others also of Indian descent, and sometimes even create an accent. If one doesn't follow the group with these activities, one is considered a "fake Indian."

Eric Ma (2002a, 2002b) tells the story of young men in Hong Kong who use rap music and the dress and style of hip hop culture, culture and music created in the urban African American communities of the US, in order to address their own urban experience, what it means to be young, male, and unemployed as one of the world's most dynamic cities rides an economic crisis.

Arun Saldanha (2002) tells the story of elite youth in Bangalore, India, who cruise the streets of the city in luxury cars playing the latest Western pop hits on the car stereo system. The car becomes a self-enclosed mobile bubble of transnational cosmopolitanism while the dark glass of its windows reflects the poverty of the city and its inhabitants back on themselves.

I'll tell you one more story, a sixth one, and that is my own. I was born in the US, but spent all my pre-teen years in Southeast Asia, South Asia, and the Middle East. Since returning to the US as a teenager, I've constantly had to reconcile that experience with the expectations and experiences of those around me. In the US, I *looked* much like my classmates (that is, white, from English, Scottish, and Central European stock), but *thought* much differently. Though I am a US citizen (related, at least according to family stories, to Martha Washington), I do not consider myself an "American" in any easy sense.

These stories are stories of the struggle for identity; to find out for oneself who one is, and to be that in the face of what everyone else seems to think you should be. These are stories of a struggle with the idea that one can only be one thing or the other; that there is a choice, and that one can choose to be authentic this or authentic that, or not. These are stories which are not new, but I feel are growing in frequency worldwide. These are stories of people in a particular place, at a particular time, who are dealing with the legacies of other places and other times. We could state that these are stories of globalization, and they are, though they seem much more personal than the issues usually addressed around that trendy term. But most of all these are stories of culture, of the realm of meanings, traditions, and experiences; of the frameworks through which people make sense of their lives and how parents, friends, and people on the street seek to shape that framework. These are stories of culture in a global time.

The anthropologist Arjun Appadurai (1996) gave us a very productive image by which we could imagine the complexities of globalization. Globalization is not a single process, happening everywhere in
the same way. Globalization is made up of a series of processes, some
of which are working in opposite directions and with opposite ends.
These processes are all about movement: that of people; of media images
and products; of technologies and industries; of money and finance;
and of political ideologies. Others have added to the list: the movement of religious ideas, of academic theories, and so on. Appadurai
imagines these processes as landscapes, so we can imagine a landscape of people, some moving and some standing still, some moving
voluntarily, some out of necessity, some at gunpoint, and we see some
embedded in a particular landscape for generations. Or we could
picture a landscape of media images and products: Hollywood films;
Bollywood films (from Bombay); and Hong Kong films, all circulating
on certain paths, appearing in certain venues, and moving on.

This is not a book that addresses things on the scale that Appadurai
(and most of the rest who speak of such issues) does. Rather, this is
a book about where these processes impinge on everyday life. This
is not about globalization in the abstract or about culture or identity in the abstract. It is about the process of trying to negotiate,
personally, with these pressures and ideas. This is a book about
dilemmas, but not a book about solutions; it is a book about posing
the sorts of questions that at least make us realize that, for example,
we're being forced to choose what we are.

The first question we have to ask is "what is culture?"

Culture

*Culture is one of the two or three most complicated words in the
English language.*

(Williams, 1983, p. 87)

The idea of culture is key to this book, because it is, after all, about
cultural globalization and not just globalization. Culture is a word that
is both powerful and ubiquitous. It is also fairly vague and can be used
to mean a variety of quite contradictory things. But it is important

for us to begin this book with something of a theoretical frame, a perspective or way of thinking about culture that connects it to our everyday lives and shows us how we can be so connected globally.

This book is something of a journey through the landscape of global culture. Like any journey it is partial because one follows a particular path and not another, one visits one place and not another, and so on. The purpose of this first chapter on culture is to pick up some traveling companions for the trip in the form of a series of concepts which, in different ways, become linked. Not all will be useful at every stop of the journey, but they help us to be prepared for what we may encounter. The companions go by the names of culture, habitus, territory, power, identity, popular culture, ideology, and hegemony. They'll be wearing name tags for a while to help keep them all straight. But this is neither an innocent conceptual toolbox nor a random assortment of concepts. It is not even a survey of concepts related to culture or globalization that one might find in a traditional textbook. This assemblage of concepts is a particular way of thinking about culture and identity which I feel is especially useful in a globalized culture. The rest of the book is basically an argument for the usefulness (or usability) of this framework and how it raises necessary questions which are important now.

First (following Raymond Williams) a brief detour through English history to try to explain what we mean when we say "culture." Before the Industrial Revolution, culture meant the tending of natural growth, like plants or animals (hence our term, "agriculture"). When applied to humans is came to mean the process of human development such as training and growth. Culture was a process, one was cultivated. With the turn of the nineteenth century, culture became a thing in and of itself. It was used to stand for the end result of the processes of cultivation. A person had culture if they had been appropriately trained and educated. But the term was also thought more broadly to mean "the general state of intellectual development, in a society as a whole" (Williams, 1961, p. 16). Culture became synonymous with civilization. It came to describe what was thought of as a general, universal process of human development and the results of that process. These results were the cultural products that were evidence of being civilized: music, art, literature, and so on. Culture was then the embodiment of a tradition and a history, the artistic record of a society. But Williams reminds us that tradition is selective; what is selected to be part of this Great Tradition, as it is sometimes called, consists of very specific items that service a social ideal. And so, therefore, for over a hundred years what was considered culture was the works of white males, usually those from the educated classes. In European writings culture was seen as an ideal that Europe had achieved but other countries were found wanting. At the height of colonialism, culture became a means of comparison, if not moral evaluation, of the supposed worth of a group of people.

There was another development around this time that helped to emphasize this particular elitist view of culture, and that was the growth of mass culture brought about by the industrialization of printing (resulting in cheap newspapers) and the increase in literacy among the working classes as the result of a new push for popular education. The idea of culture as a moral evaluation was applied to these new developments. And so, within a society, Britain for example, you had two different cultures: High culture, which embodied the ideals of the nation (associated with high art, philosophy, and education) and low culture (or mass culture), which is what the bulk of the population consumed. These latter texts, songs, and artworks were decidedly not considered to embody the ideals of the society, but to be mere trash. In fact, according to how the term had been used, these latter texts, songs, and artworks were not considered "culture" at all. This distinction between high and low culture was then used to make a moral judgment of the people that consumed them. If you read the great works, the argument goes, you will become refined. If you read trashy novels, you yourself become trashy; you became one of the "masses."

This distinction still exists today, but to a lesser extent than before. But back in the 1950s, when Williams began writing about culture, the distinction was still very much in place and Williams took the dismissal of the greater part of the population as mere uncultured, ignorant, worthless masses personally. He took it personally because he had grown up in a working class family in Wales, had received a scholarship, and had studied at Oxford. He realized that the so-called "masses" who were being so easily degraded and dismissed in the teashops and lecture halls of Oxford were his family and friends, and he felt insulted. To treat any group of people, as a whole, as if they had uncritical minds and no means of creating culture, was untenable to Williams. And so he proposed the fairly simple concept that culture was ordinary. What he meant by this was that the processes of culture, which were the inheritance of a tradition and also the testing of that inheritance within the context of one's everyday life, did not just occur with certain peoples or works, but were the basic processes of everyone's everyday lives. They were normal processes. They were ordinary.

Indulge me for a moment and let me quote Williams at length because he says these things much better than I:

> Culture is ordinary: that is the first fact. Every human society has its own shape, its own purposes, its own meanings. Every human society expresses these, in institutions, and in arts and learning. The making of a society is the finding of common meanings and directions, and its growth is an active debate and amendment under the pressures of experience, contact, and discovery, writing themselves into the land. The growing society is there, yet it is also made and remade in every individual mind. The making of a mind is, first, the slow learning of shapes, purposes, and meanings, so that work, observation, and communication are possible. Then, second, but equal in importance, is the testing of these in experience, the making of new observations, comparisons, and meanings. A culture has two aspects: the known meanings and directions, which its members are trained to; the new observations and meanings, which are offered and tested. These are the ordinary processes of human societies and human minds, and we see through them the nature of a culture: that it is always both traditional and creative; that it is both the most ordinary common meanings and the finest individual meanings. We use the word culture in these two senses: to mean a whole way of life – the common meanings; to mean the arts and learning – the special processes of discovery and creative effort. Some writers reserve the word for one or the other of these senses; I insist on both, and on the significance of their conjunction. The questions I ask about our culture are questions about our general and common purposes, yet also questions about deep personal meanings. Culture is ordinary, in every society and in every mind. (Williams, 1989, p. 4)

By arguing this, however, Williams is not arguing for a cultural relativism: that all cultures are equally valuable and that we cannot make any judgments of artistic value. He writes, later in the same essay, that "[a]t home we met and made music, listened to it, recited and listened to poems, valued fine language. I have heard better music and better poems since; there is the world to draw on" (p. 5). What he is arguing *against* is the a priori dismissal of people and their culture, and what he is arguing *for* is the recognition that there are many, many other ways of making meaning, many other traditions, and many ways of testing, shaping, and challenging those meanings and traditions. In fact, he is not simply arguing that the elite should recognize the culture of the working classes, but that everyone should recognize the richness of their common cultures. The key to accomplishing this goal is education. Education, Williams writes, is ordinary: "that it is, before everything else, the process of giving to the ordinary members of society its full common meanings, and the skills that will enable them to amend these meanings, in the light of their personal and common experience" (p. 14). In other words, to give people the resources they need to understand the range of common cultures and the means to change these in light of their own experience. That is, to recognize that one has options (that the world is a wide place, and that there are other poems and songs, some better and some not) and to provide some of the tools necessary to engage more directly in the forces (social, political, and cultural) that shape one's everyday life.

There are some problems with Williams' argument that need to be addressed before we can move on. And one of these is the reason that I have not been entirely true to Williams in the above summary. Williams writes of the common culture, and I write of the common cultures. If culture is a whole way of life, whose way of life dominates? If the goal is a common culture, whose culture becomes common? Indeed, historian E. P. Thompson (1961) revised Williams' phrase to argue that culture is a "whole way of struggle."

Another issue is the amorphous nature of a "whole way of life." How does one distinguish between one person's whole way of life and another's? What distinguishes one culture from another? Any two cultures will have some things in common, and some things different. What counts as a whole way of life? Can an individual have a culture that is not in some way shared with others? If so, do we lose any sense of common culture and end up back in a cultural relativism? As a means of convenience, we often use demographic categories to mark distinctions between cultures. So there are cultural differences because of race and ethnicity, class, gender, sexual orientation, geographical location, generation, etc. However, which of these categories matter at any particular place and time are culturally and historically contingent. Williams, for example, foregrounds class differences and ignores differences in ethnicity. In the US, on the other hand, ethnic and racial differences tend to get emphasized and class gets shorter shrift. But while it may be convenient to talk about the differences, for example in the US context, between Northern culture and Southern culture, we can never predict from that the meanings, life experience, or even culture of any particular individual within those areas.

It's a bit of a mess. As I said, it's a difficult concept. But for now I want to hang on to the general sense of culture as being a whole way of life, that is culture as the ordinary processes of meaning making, of traditions, and creativity. And we also need to recognize the two-sided, processual nature of culture as we discuss particular cultures in different parts of the world and their struggles between tradition and change. Culture is always dynamic, traditions will always change, but we also need to recognize that there might be things to hang on to from a tradition while at the same time acknowledging that just because something is a tradition doesn't mean that it should continue. It is not my goal in this book to provide the reader with a set of criteria for making these decisions, but rather to set out examples of these processes and hopefully the means to recognize these processes in other contexts and the impetus to find the resources necessary for that situation to make an honest judgment about these decisions and processes.

These then are some of the issues regarding the idea of culture more generally. However, we will be spending time in a particular realm of culture, popular culture, which I need to say a word about here. The terms *popular culture* and *mass culture* are often confused. Mass culture refers to cultural products that are mass produced (like CDs). Popular culture is often thought of as culture that is popular (that is, that many people purchase or participate in), but a better way of thinking about it is that popular culture is culture that people themselves have made, rather than culture that is made for them. This distinction is one emphasized by communication scholar John Fiske (1989, p. 25): "Popular culture is made by the people at the interface between the products of the culture industries and everyday life." It is, in part, what we do with the mass media products once we have obtained them. Most of the time products are used in the ways that their manufacturers intended, but not always. For example, producers of vinyl record albums assumed that their products would be simply listened to and did not intend their products to be "scratched" to *make* music (rap). Likewise, Diet Coke may make an excellent beverage, but it is also claimed to remove rust efficiently as well (indeed, there are volumes out there on cleaning tips where common household items are used in ways their designers never imagined).

But when we say that popular culture is "what we do" with the products, part of what we do with them is make meaning. Meaning is not inherent in a text, but has to be produced. Much of the time the audience will all make roughly the same meaning of a text, and that meaning will be roughly what the producers meant that text to be, but not always. It is always possible to "read" a cultural text in a very different, even oppositional, way. Fiske (1989, p. 25) provides the following example:

> Young urban Aborigines in Australia watching old Westerns on Saturday-morning television ally themselves with the Indians, cheer them on as they attack the wagon train or homestead, killing the white men and carrying off the white women: they also identify with Arnold, the eternal black child in a white paternalist family in *Diff'rent Strokes* – constructing allegiances among American blackness, American Indianness, and Australian Aboriginality that enable them to make their sense out of their experience of being nonwhite in a white society.

We can think of this resistant reading as the creative challenge Williams posits as part of the ordinary processes of culture. This does not mean that one can read anything into anything or make anything mean whatever you wish it to (as Humpty Dumpty once said to Alice). Popular culture is always both the dominant uses and meanings and at least the potential for alternative uses and readings. Popular culture is, therefore, a site of ideological struggle more generally and personal struggle as one searches for one's place in family, tradition, and society at large. Popular culture becomes a way of bending the meanings of mass culture and everyday life to help oneself on one's way. Fiske borrows a term from French sociologist Michel de Certeau (1984) and writes that popular culture is "the art of making do," which looks at acts of cultural resistance and containment. Often this resistance is not that of one who wishes to bring down the entire system, but the resistance of one who wishes to make it through a space controlled by others (school, work, the streets, home) in a way that makes life bearable and which maintains one's identity as much as possible. The aboriginal youths mentioned in the example above do not change the films they watch, or the dominant economic system that produced them, but they draw from the films a moment of resistance and identity. In the end, however, the Indians are defeated and the youths are counted as just more audience members contributing to a ratings share for a broadcast company. Do these acts of popular resistance make a difference? They do to the youths who perform them.

Now it is time to meet some of our other conceptual companions.

Territory

If culture is a whole way of life, how do we negotiate and make our way through that life? I want to borrow (and transform) a term from the French sociologist Pierre Bourdieu in order to give us the means to answer this question. The term is *habitus*, which Bourdieu (1990) defines as the "feel for the game" that one has, the game being everyday life at a particular place and time. Habitus is the set of things that you do to cope with life and with other people, to make it in your own culture or to deal with other cultures when you encounter them. We could consider habitus as a sort of style that one has, and we can mean this both literally as what you wear (to fit in, or not; to identify oneself with a group, or not) and more broadly as how you act (what language you use, what distance you keep). Habitus is the set of styles that we have developed to help us move in and out of groups of people, different spaces (home, work, school, street, mall), and different life worlds. I should note that habitus is not just a set of personally learned habits, but, as James Lull (1995, p. 69) has defined it, "a system of socially learned cultural predispositions and activities," that is, a set of social strategies that one learns (and then adopts and adapts). I introduce this term first because I want to plant the image of a person moving through a social space (public or private) before I start talking about territory and territorialization.

Territory is perhaps, along with culture, the key term in this book. Cultural globalization needs to be understood, I argue, through a theory of culture, territory, and identity. I have a fairly specific meaning for territory that I will be using here. A territory is an area of influence that one has. Everyone marks a territory. Dogs and birds mark territory and nations mark territory. Territory is that area in which you have power and influence. Both individuals and groups have territories. Your territory is your space, your turf. In your territory, particular social rules apply (Lull, 1995), and you act differently. For example, a teacher in front of a class may mark their territory by dressing a certain way, arranging the furniture in a certain way, and they behave in a certain way (facing the room, for example) that gives them control of that space. Within a classroom, specific social rules apply (raise your hand and be recognized before speaking, take notes of what is said, pay attention), and the particular teacher may add more rules (no cell phones in class, sit in straight lines).

When we walk through different neighborhoods we encounter other territories, groups of people who mark their space in particular ways: the music changes, people interact differently, the street and shop signs may even switch languages, and so on. Gangs mark territory by means of graffiti. Someone who is playing music connects with others who like that music. As topics of conversation change, groups of interest form and break up (for example, if I begin to ramble on about a particular television show, I will suddenly interest one part of the audience but bore another, who will tune out). There are also smoking territories, usually just outside the entrances to buildings, in which communities are formed, and space marked, by the practice of lighting up.

Identity

Each territory draws on a culture, but is not completely representative of that culture. There is a general culture of smokers (created by the dual forces of social stigma and coolness factor), but each group (outside a classroom building, next to the bus stop, outside the expensive restaurant) will have different dynamics. Likewise, consider the example of an exchange student from Russia studying in the US. That student's room may draw on elements of Russian culture to territorialize, to say something about who they are. But this does not mean that this particular space is representative of all of Russia or that this individual's tastes, interpretations, and behaviors could be seen as somehow purely Russian. Each territory may draw on elements from diverse cultures and inflect them in a particular way. Those cultural elements used to mark territory (and identity), are also those that make it possible to move through and live in society (in other words, they are your habitus).

Territories are more or less ephemeral. They have to be continually maintained. Some territories are marked by physical impediments (style of architecture) which make them more permanent. But many others are created through symbols and habits, and these change. We can think of the range of our identity markers: the sprawl of our body, the drape of a coat, a haze of smoke, the range of sound, posters, pictures, furniture, knick-knacks, colors, pets, stuff. All these things create an expressive space. What that space expresses is me. I am constructed in the process of this expression. This is not a fully conscious and intentional process; we are not fully aware or deliberate in what we're doing. We just arrange spaces until they feel right. But this is not a rationalist view of the self because much of this process is done by habit. Some of these habits are personal (the idiosyncratic tics, repetitions, and predilections of each of us) and some are habits of culture. Personal habits are the ways I do certain things without thinking; cultural habits are the ways *we* do certain things without thinking, with the "we" referring to others in the relevant culture. It's also not voluntarist because one is always territorializing with the means at one's disposal and these vary drastically by income, location, chance, class, and so on. We often say that we want our personal spaces to express who we are, to express me. And this is true in the following regard: our identity is not only expressed but constituted by these territories. My identity does not exist prior to territorialization. What this raises is the tricky philosophical problem of deconstructing the notion that each of us has a single, coherent, stable identity, or "I." As the French philosopher Gilles Deleuze likes to say, there is no I, just the habit of saying "I." There is no self, just the continual process of territorializing to express self, to search for self.

I want to emphasize this link between the processes of territorialization and processes of identity. Identity is part of one's own self-formation, but also the consequence of what groups and others impose on one. The concept of identity as territorialization allows us to rework cultural debates about identity. Let us quickly set out four ideas of identity to help clarify this. *Essentialist* views on identity state that groups have authentic, natural identities and characteristics, which trap them and leave them unable to change. Biology is destiny. An example of an essentialist view of identity is the argument for the biological basis for race. This view states that races are essentially and, therefore, absolutely different because of biological differences like appearance or DNA. This view has been scientifically disproved: there is no biological basis for racial difference. Indeed, there is more genetic variation within the so-called races than between them. What we call races are culturally constructed categories that vary tremendously from place to place. Different cultures will split the population up in different ways. Black, for example, refers to different groups of people in the US, UK, and South Africa. In the US, at the turn of the previous century, the Irish were not considered "white." An essentialist territorialization would see particular ways of living, particular spaces and habits, as being determined by your essential characteristics (race, gender, and so on). Your "true self" is your genetic heritage.

The next position, then, is the *antiessentialist* position which argues that there are *no* biological bases for identity. For example, just because two individuals are both biologically female does not mean that both will necessarily share the same traits, thoughts, abilities, attitudes, interests, and so on. Therefore, one cannot make blanket universal statements like "All Asians are . . ." or "All women are . . ." Now, this view vehemently does *not* argue that the social and cultural categories of race, gender, and so on, are illusions. People believe in these categories and act on them, discriminating against others. The categories may be social constructions, but they have very real, indeed deadly, effects.[1] "To think of identities as interchangeable or infinitely open does violence to the historical and social constraints imposed on us by structures of exploitation and privilege. But to posit innate and immobile identities for ourselves or others confuses history with nature, and denies the possibility of change" (Lipsitz, 1994, p. 62).

These theories are relevant here because they represent important dimensions of our lives. Immigrant populations get trapped within these essentialist frameworks that set up expectations for behavior, intelligence, criminality, and so on. It is important to struggle against essentialist views of identity – they limit the creativity and perceived abilities allowed to people. In a globalized world it is more important than ever to assert that not all men are alike, or women, or black people, or Asians, or . . . you get the idea.

However, there are times when, politically and strategically, an appeal to an essentialist identity is useful. For example, if one is struggling against patriarchy (the social domination of women by men), arguing that all women are different and have nothing in common means that it is difficult for women to find common ground on which to organize and mount a response to patriarchy. So one claims an *essential* identity *strategically* (stating that, for example, despite all our differences, we are all women). What's called *strategic essentialism* is a way of expressing an "essential identity" which isn't really essential (because we are all hybrids), but it's important to express that identity at a particular time and place (strategic) perhaps to connect with a larger group for political gain and a louder voice. For example, the African continent is quite diverse culturally, socially, politically, environmentally, ethnically, and musically. We cannot speak of "African Music" as a whole. However, if African musicians want to make their presence known on the world stage, claiming "African" identity makes one part of a much larger group than simply a national or tribal identity can. "Africans" speak with a louder voice that "Kenyans" because they are in greater numbers. There are dangers to this strategy because it plays into a Western conception that all Africans are alike. Strategic essentialism then is a political move which claims that a hybrid territory is culturally pure for strategic gain.

George Lipsitz describes a fourth strategy, what he terms *strategic antiessentialism*, which has particular relevance for our discussions in this book. Strategic antiessentialism means taking on another identity (not essential to one's self), a mask or disguise. This shows that identity is not essential since one can become (or at least appear to become) something one is not. But this practice is *strategic* because one is doing so mainly to express something about oneself which one cannot express in one's current identity. Whereas with strategic essentialism one focuses on and claims one aspect of one's identity, with strategic antiessentialism one claims an identity which one is not. To do this is to take on "disguises in order to express indirectly parts of their identity that might be too threatening to express directly" (Lipsitz, 1994, p. 62). A disguise is strategically chosen, "on the basis of its ability to highlight, underscore, and augment an aspect of one's identity that one can not express directly" (p. 62). Those who utilize this strategy "see how they can become 'more themselves' by appearing to be something other than themselves" (p. 63).

One example that Lipsitz uses is that of the Mardi Gras Indians in New Orleans. The Mardi Gras Indians are groups of African American men who create Native American tribal identities and fanciful Native American costumes and march and dance in Mardi Gras parades. Lipsitz writes that these groups "enact vulgar and vicious stereotypes of Native Americans that resonate more with the history of Wild West shows and Hollywood Westerns than with the actual historical experiences of Native peoples" (p. 71). The musical group The Neville Brothers is perhaps the most famous of these participants, presenting themselves as part of the Wild Tchoupitoulas and recording songs for the parades. But their assumption of these stereotypical identities has a number of strategic purposes. For example, it is illegal for Black people to wear masks in New Orleans and so by painting their faces instead they can obscure their identities while retaining a presence in the public space of the parade. Also, though stereotypical, the costumes remind the crowd of the nation's history of treatment of Native Americans (in some ways an expression of the social and economic oppression of African Americans). The performances allow these men to vent their anger at their conditions, but indirectly, in ways which are not allowed them in daily life. They also bring the Black community together while problematizing simple notions of racial identity (Black Indians). "By pretending to be something other than 'Black' for a day, the Mardi Gras Indians bring to the surface all the more powerfully their Caribbean and African ancestries" (p. 72).

Identity is always caught up in competing forces of territorialization. Territorialization is actually two processes: deterritorialization and reterritorialization. To *deterritorialize* is to erase or suppress the markers of a territory. This can come in the form of a prohibition: a sign reading "no radios on the beach" prevents any one group from dominating that public space via music and lyrics; school dress codes prevent the territorialization of gangs and social cliques; graffiti is painted over; and so on. It can also come from taking logos off clothes and shoes. But to deterritorialize can also mean taking oneself out of a territory. This can be understood literally as moving to another location, or experientially like when one tunes out a dull professor or listens to music on an iPod or connects with friends and relatives in other places via the Internet, text messaging, or mobile phone use.

Reterritorialization is the imposition of a territory on another area (already territorialized). An example could be driving through a neighborhood playing loud music in your car. The music shapes the territory of the street. To reterritorialize means to rework the cultural symbols that are in place, using them in different ways. This could be repainting the walls of the house you just purchased to reflect your own aesthetics: one paints over the old color scheme and imposes a new one.

Deterritorialization and reterritorialization are not separate processes, and each can be used to both control and resist control in social spaces. They can be seen as ways of controlling the identities possible in a space, and as ways of reinserting one's identity into a different space. But not all practices of territorialization are equal. Territorialization is always about the exercise of *power*: the power of an institution to control a space, and the power of individuals and groups to elude control (cf. de Certeau, 1984). This power is unequally distributed in society. Just because someone territorializes by tagging a wall with graffiti doesn't make them as powerful as the institution that built that wall. A relevant example of territorialization is that of English-only laws in the US, that is the insistence that English be the only language spoken in public schools. These laws can be seen as attempts to maintain a broader cultural identity by reinforcing rules of language use, tied to cultural expression. It is an example of an institution (or series of them) exercising power on immigrant communities.

There are a number of types of power. James Lull (1995), following John B. Thompson, points out that there is economic power (the one with the most gold wins), political power (the ability to influence policy and social government), coercive power (might makes right), and symbolic or cultural power. Note that these types of power do not necessarily coincide. Just because one has a lot of political influence doesn't necessarily make one wealthy (and vice versa). Through their influence on students, teachers can be said to have tremendous cultural power, but very little economic, political, or coercive power (especially since one cannot use corporal punishment in the classroom anymore). It is the realm of symbolic or cultural power that most interests us here, though the other forms of power will have obvious relevance. Lull (1995, p. 72) discusses cultural power this way: "[C]ultural power reflects how, in the situated realms of everyday life, individuals and groups construct and declare their cultural identities and activities and how those expressions and behaviors influence others."

Cultural power could be the power that a peer group has on your own identity, or perhaps the influence of a charismatic or trendsetting peer. Cultural power is also found in the creation of cultural products or texts (music, images, and so on) that millions use to territorialize and shape who they are. Note, anecdotally, the ways that the bored doodle drawings of children have taken on more of the aesthetic of Japanese anime in recent years (the type of line used, the shape of figures and features). As Lull writes, cultural power is also "the ability to define a situation culturally" (p. 71). As an example of this, Lull points out the cultural influence of black popular culture in the US: music, style, and influential personages (from Oprah to Michael Jordan). Hip hop as a style and rap as a musical form have given many worldwide a form through which to express their own identities (more on this later in the book). As Lipsitz (1994, p. 33) has put it, they have "established new centers of cultural power from Kingston, Jamaica to Compton, California." But just because black popular culture has some power, this does not translate into economic, political, or coercive power for African Americans in general (though it does allow a few to become quite wealthy). This is pointed out by Lipsitz: "At a time when African people have less power and fewer resources than at almost any previous time in history, African culture has emerged as the single most important subtext within world popular culture" (p. 36). For generations the cultural creativity of black culture has been used as a source of economic power for the white majority (for example the appropriation of predominantly black r&b into predominantly white rock and roll, or the rhythms and music of Africa being used as sources of inspiration for Western artists like Paul Simon, Malcolm McLaren, and Peter Gabriel).

The struggles apparent in our tour of cultural globalization are often struggles over cultural power, and the ability (and inability) of translating between one type of power and another (to advocate for political or economic change). If we consider identity as a territorializing move, then the ability to produce those items that get used to territorialize is an important one indeed. But we should not think of this as a direct influence and we should not think of individuals as being so passive in this process. One has the ability to choose what one uses to territorialize and also what those items will mean within their own context. Popular culture, as discussed earlier, is the case in point here.

Home

This process of shaping spaces, uses, and meanings to create and maintain identity, to create and maintain a space of comfort, is a process of making home (or home-making). I want to distinguish this process from the idea of "the home" which is more of a specific place (one's house, apartment, room). The home that one lives in may not be a place of comfort, but the activities that one pursues to create a space of comfort within the place of the home is what I want to refer to as *home*. If we consider home to be a far away place (as do people living overseas on business who return for "home leave"; or immigrants who think of home as being another country from the one where they currently live), what we are doing is territorializing, with that longing for home as being part of the home-making process. Such processes often get overlaid with notions of nostalgia for other places and other times, but that will vary depending on the specifics of a situation. We see this sort of conflict in the earlier example from Sunaina Marr Maira and the different groups of second generation Indian young adults, some of whom develop this nostalgia for Mother India (and make it an essential part of their territory, identity, and home), and others who are quite content to be American (though may still include parts of Indian culture in their home-making processes).

As I wrote a number of years ago on the idea of home:

Home can be a collection of objects, furniture, and so on that one carries with oneself from move to move. Home is the feeling that comes when the final objects are unpacked and arranged and the space seems complete (or even when one stares at the unpacked boxes, imagining). The markers of home, however, are not simply inanimate objects (a place with stuff), but the presence, habits, and effects of spouses, children, parents, companions. One can be at home simply in the presence of a significant other. What makes home territories different from other territories is on the one hand the living of the territory ... and on the other their connection with identity, or rather a process of identification. ... Homes, we feel, arc ours. (Wise, 2003, p. 111)

As Svetlana Boym (1994, p. 166) has put it, when discussing a visit back to the St Petersburg apartment in which she had grown up, "it was not the space itself, not the house, but the way of inhabiting it that had made it a home ..."

The process of home-making is a cultural one in that it is a process of meaning making, of traditions and experience. We draw on cultural meanings, habits, practices, and objects in making our spaces of comfort. In this notion of home we can see the intersection of our discussions of culture, habitus, identity, territory, power, and popular culture. We might more properly call this intersection of concepts and practices an *assemblage*. An assemblage is a heterogeneous collection of people and things (Wise, 2005). These collections of things are both structured (by families, societies, cultures, and institutions) and contingent (relying on the availability of resources, individual intention, and chance). But the assemblage is not just a person and his or her things but the relation among all these things, the qualities of these things, their meanings and ideas, habits, rhythms. The idea of assemblage incorporates as well the processes of de- and reterritorialization. In fact, assemblages are always processes – home is the process of making a space of comfort, identity is the process of searching for itself. Cultural globalization is the process of assemblage making (and unmaking).

Let me give you an example which ties together some of these threads and connects them back to the idea of identity. This is the example of Third Culture Kids (TCKs, also called Global Nomads, Expatriate

Adolescents, and other terms). This is a personal example in that I fit the profile of a TCK. A TCK is defined as:

> a person who has spent a significant part of his or her developmental years outside the parents' culture. The TCK builds relationships to all of the cultures, while not having full ownership in any. Although elements from each culture are assimilated into the TCK's life experience, the sense of belonging is in relationship to others of similar background. (Pollock and Van Reken, 1999, p. 19)

To a certain extent my own experience of growing up in a variety of countries is what inspired me to teach some of the subjects I do and to eventually write this book. The spaces I grew up in were always crossroads between the culture of my American parents and the cultures of the country where we were living. I would notice how different families in similar situations would territorialize according to different strategies. I remember walking in to houses of friends of mine from school and getting an overwhelming feeling of Americanness, or Indianness, or Britishness from the stuff in the house and the way the house was inhabited. From inside their confines the outside world didn't matter – one could be in India, Korea, the Philippines, or Milwaukee. Other houses reflected mixtures of places and cultures; some contained a myriad assortment of objects which were the traces of that family's various postings. Our houses were more of the latter. The walls always seemed relatively culturally permeable.

Moving from country to country as a child, each of these different territories made an impression on my own territorializations. But I am not a pure product of any of them. The third culture of the child in these circumstances is one created in the spaces where parent culture and local culture intersect. TCKs seem picture perfect examples of antiessentialist views of identity, and TCK identity can also be seen as an assemblage of people, places, things, languages, and so on.

The wheels fall off the wagon somewhat when we begin to look at the burgeoning literature on TCKs (e.g., Ender, 2002; Pollock and Van Reken, 1999; Smith, 1991, 1996). The problem is that in this literature the third culture tends to become an essentialized identity, but one constructed through the processes of cultural hybridity (making it more a strategic essentialism). The assumption is made that the experience of being a TCK gives them (us) a set of standard characteristics (frequently mobile as adults, achieving high levels of education, international focus and outlook, good with languages, good at mediating conflicts, inclined to depression, and so on). Indeed, it is an oft-cited statement of being a TCK that TCKs have more in common with other TCKs than with those in their "home" cultures. Now, I can understand this statement as a desire for affiliation, that is, since it is a pretty lonely existence (who else is constituted by these particular cultures, histories, and trajectories who can understand where one is coming from?) finding others who understand and who have similar experiences is important. This is especially true when one returns to one's parents' home culture, except for one it's just a new country, not a return home. Returning "home" can prove quite alienating.

There may be superficial similarities between TCKs, but how deep do these go (Hylmo, 2002)? A desire for common identity is part of the desire for community. The desire for community allows one to evade real, deep, cultural and experiential differences (especially ones having to do with differences in power). An American child growing up in Bangladesh, a Ugandan in London, and a Peruvian in Turkey may share a type of experience, but the economic and political dimensions of their home assemblages may produce significant differences as well. TCK experience is an important one to pay attention to if we want to understand cultural globalization, but only if we keep in mind the material realities of their territorializations – TCKs encompass the elite capitalist and diplomatic class, the military, the missionary, the impoverished refugee, the aid worker, and so on.

The identity of TCKs assumed by the literature, a literature that tends to focus on examples of Americans abroad and that tends to exclude the experience of refugees and impoverished immigrant families and children, is that of a self-enclosed bubble of global consciousness, detached from the particulars of place. Sara Ahmed (1999, p. 338), in her critique of some of this literature, writes:

> The very detachment from a particular home grants the nomadic subject the ability to see the world: an ability that becomes the basis for a new global identity and community. In such a narrative, identity becomes fetishized: it becomes detached from the particularity of places which allow for its formation as such.

In my description and theorization of home above, I do not reduce home to such a detached interiorization, but see it as a process of dealing with spaces both at hand and distant. Identity in such a model is always already in process, shaped by economic and political forces, the historical realities of one's territories. We need to pay attention to TCK experience, but we must define the category and theorize that experience more carefully, with more nuance, and I think the concept of culture and territory and identity helps.

There are two more traveling companions to introduce before we move on in our journey: ideology and hegemony.

Ideology and Hegemony

Processes of making do, and of making home, occur within frameworks of assumptions known as ideologies. An *ideology* is a system of ideas that are taken for granted. By system of ideas, I mean that an ideology consists of the articulation of a number of ideas. For example, "freedom" by itself is not an ideology; ideology is the connection of "freedom" with other ideas (Hall, 1981, p. 31). In the West freedom is articulated to ideas of the individual (so we think of individual freedoms), but in more collectivist countries freedom is articulated to ideas of the group (so freedom is freedom for the society not the individual; a notion which seems hard to grasp in the West). These assumptions are taken for granted, almost unconscious. As British cultural studies scholar Stuart Hall has explained, whenever you hear yourself stating that something is "obvious" or "natural" or that "it's just the way things are" or "the way things should be" or when something just seems "common sense," then we are dealing with ideology. Ideology is the filter and framework through which we interpret our world. When we use ideology in this way it is not something that is false (one has false ideas in one's head) because that implies that there is a "true" way of viewing the world. It is also not a relativism, meaning I am not arguing that all interpretations and ways of viewing the world are inherently equal and correct. Some are wrong and some are dangerous.

We use the term *dominant ideology* to mean a system of ideas that is more widespread and accepted than other systems; usually this dominant system is reinforced and presented in centralized institutions (like the media, schools, courts, and laws) and represent the interests of those in power. Usually, but not always, since systems of ideas are always changing. Our assumptions about what the world means and how things should be are constantly being challenged by our own experiences in life. Those experiences may lead us to question these ideas, or they may reinforce them. But think of this: what if one could exercise cultural power so that your interests and worldview becomes the common sense of other groups? To have others accept your view of the world as common sense and natural, even if this is not in their best interests, is power indeed. We call this power *hegemony*. Hegemony is the act of consent on the part of a population to unquestioningly accept the view of the world presented by dominant institutions, even if this view works against the well-being and best interests of the population. For example, to get people to vote for tax cuts because it seems the right thing to do, even if those cuts end up defunding education and other social support institutions (like healthcare and welfare) to the detriment of those same people and their children, is hegemony. The key term of hegemony is "consent." The consent of the population is never something that is guaranteed and fixed, it is always a struggle and always has to be reinforced and renewed.

Orientalism

Orientalism is an ideology of relevance to our project here. It is based on the assumption that there is a clear, essential, and absolute difference between the West and the East (the Orient). It is assumed that Oriental people and cultures have certain essential traits: primitive, obedient, mysterious, spiritual, wise, exotic, despotic, crafty, devious, barbaric, ancient, and so on. The construction of this assemblage of ideas about the Orient was a European invention which was both produced by and justified European colonialism (Said, 1979).[2] If the Orient was primitive and barbaric, then it was up to the enlightened West to civilize and tame it, and at the same time rescue and preserve the ancient knowledge and wisdom held by the great traditions of the East.

Orientalism isn't just a set of ideas, it isn't just discourse or mere ideology. This is because it was an ideology crafted and sponsored by particular institutions (universities, banks, companies, armies, governments) with the economic, political, and coercive power to act on it (having guns, boats, money, armies, merchant fleets, and did I say guns?). What is also important is that Orientalism isn't a rejection of the Orient but a particular appreciation of it – it sponsors the study of Eastern cultures (within the Orientalist framework) and produces knowledge about Eastern peoples, religions, traditions, and histories which is then accepted as the true knowledge of these places and peoples (this is part of its insidious nature). There is then something called *self-orientalism* where people from these cultures accept and embrace this conception of themselves (India is spiritual, China is Confucian, and so on). There is not, however, a true reverse-Orientalism (or Occidentalism) though there have been attempts to essentialize the West (not to mention the fact that by defining itself in contrast to the Orient, the West has already essentialized itself in the formulation of Orientalism). The reason for this is that Occidentalist thought generally lacks the power and material infrastructure to carry itself out to the extent that Orientalism has done over the past few centuries.

Any project that studies globalization must be wary of Orientalism, that is essentializing the Other. This is especially true when Westerners write with authority on non-Western matters. I'm not arguing that they (we) can't do it, but that one needs to be wary of the West once again speaking the Truth for the Orient in which the Orient itself is conspicuously silent. Orientalism is far from being ancient history. Egregious stereotypes of peoples from Africa, the Middle East, and Asia regularly cross our television and film screens. In the early 1990s Samuel Huntington predicted an upcoming clash of civilizations, a formulation that essentialized the West and the East as being absolutely different and culturally and morally opposed. The terrorist attacks of 11 September, 2001 and the ensuing wars in Afghanistan and Iraq as well as the war on terrorism are often described in similarly absolutist terms: them and us, with "them" being primitive, barbaric "evil doers." As cultural critic Ziauddin Sardar (1999, pp. vii–viii) has put it, "the fact of Orientalism will always impede understanding between the East and the West. We need to begin again, from different premises, and find new bases for genuine encounters with the people, places, history, ideas and current existence that is to the East of the West."

If we look at cultural globalization from the perspective of home-making, it is about how people make sense of the world and themselves in the light of a variety of competing world views and assumptions. We hear about the struggles between local cultures and global cultures (usually meaning Western, if not American, cultures). What this book aims at is that point in everyday life when both sides of this struggle come together, where the individual draws on elements from either or both in making sense of their everyday lives. This is a moment of the everyday assemblage, the everyday processes of territorialization, of gathering oneself together, of moving through spaces and places, rooms, corridors, streets. Cultural globalization is ordinary. In this process we realize that what we might consider local or traditional culture has been a hybrid culture all along, and that the global culture that it is faced with is far from uniform or universal. Both global and local cultures are assemblages of things, meanings, peoples, each with their own trajectories, movements, and qualities. It is to the global that we now turn.

Notes

1 Paul Gilroy (1993, p. 102) puts this caveat as follows: "identity can be understood neither as a fixed essence nor as a vague and utterly contingent construction to be reinvented by the will and whim of aesthetes, symbolists, and language gamers. . . . Whatever the radical constructionists may say, [racial identity] is lived as a coherent (if not always stable) experiential sense of self. Though it is often felt to be natural and spontaneous, it remains the outcome of practical activity: language, gesture, bodily significations, desires."

2 Orientalism as a term has a long history, meaning basically the study of what was considered the East by Westerners. The term achieved its current political and critical valence through the work of Edward Said (1979). His work is certainly not uncontroversial and he does have his critics (see, e.g., Sardar, 1999, and Young, 1990, for discussions of the controversies and issues taken with Said's work).

2

Culture and the Global

Non-Local Connections

Considering this process of culture as home-making, we may begin to realize just how many of the markers and articulations that one is making are with non-local objects, people, and sites. This could range from your Tibetan Buddhist symbol tattoo, to the British band playing on the stereo, to the Australian wine chilling in the fridge, to your brother stationed at an Army base in Iraq, to an Aunt in Mexico, to the poster of a Tahitian beach. If we consider where various items were manufactured, we begin to trace the physical history of our home objects to China, Vietnam, the Philippines, Mexico, and so on. If we consider our favorite cuisines we begin to mark Chinese, Mexican, Thai, Lebanese, Cuban, Indian, and so on (and if we track those establishments through their founders and personnel we encounter more particularities: Sikh, Tamil, Taiwanese, Honduran . . .). With some thought it becomes fairly easy to map ones connections to elsewheres. Indeed, there is a version of discourse about globalization that revels in pointing out such connections, especially when they seem unusual: A touring Peruvian band mixing traditional songs and instruments with rock guitars playing a blues club in the trendy district of Seoul; a Sudanese immigrant bagging groceries in Arizona; a city park in Guangzhou, China, with a playground featuring Disney characters, and so on.

But the process of home-making is not a relativistic one; objects and articulations are not all weighted equally, and they are not all readily available. Again, there is a version of globalization, which we will discuss below, that sees globalization as being filled with these relativistic connections: the whole world seems available everywhere (look at all the spices available in your local supermarket, they argue; look at all the ethnic foods!). Cultures are borrowing, diversifying, connecting. Couscous, apparently, is the favorite dish of the French, and Japan and China love pizza, and Indians enjoy going out for Chinese food (Pidd, 2007). What the relativistic version of these processes neglects in the nature of these connections; it neglects the key issue of *power*.

Doreen Massey discusses the geography of a culture as consisting of interconnections that cross multiple spaces. She writes, "The interconnections which bind together and internally differentiate a diaspora culture, for instance, cut across regions, nation states and continents, linking local areas in, say, a British city to a Turkish region of Cyprus, to a particular island in the Caribbean or a village in India" (Massey, 1998, p. 124). These interconnections form "constellations of temporary coherence . . . set within a social space which is the product of relations and interconnections from the very local to the intercontinental" (pp. 124–5, emphasis removed). To better think these interconnections, Massey uses a generative pun. Rather than thinking of culture as *roots*, as peoples belonging to particular places and traditions and practices, we need to think of culture as *routes*, as the movements of peoples, goods, ideas from place to place.[1] The process of home-making, then, is not a search for origins (where does one *really* belong?) but of tracking the ever-shifting constellations of home-markers, territories, and articulations.

What is very important for Massey is that these interconnections are actually social relations and as such have varying levels and types of power; and that power is directional. So some social relations have more cultural power than others. She points out (1998, p. 125), by means of example, that a Guatemalan child wearing a US T-shirt is not the equivalent of a US child wearing a Guatemalan T-shirt:

> When, say, young people in Guatemala sport clothing marked clearly as "from the USA" (or – ironically – with an "American" logo and trademark emblazoned upon it but in fact quite likely made in Guatemala, a T-shirt quite likely sewn up by the mother of the

Guatemalan kids themselves) they are tapping into, displaying their knowledge of, their claimed connection with, that dominant culture to the north. The social relations (both cultural and economic) embedded in this flow of cultural influence (and thus in the particular moment of the wearing of this T-shirt) are complex but they are clearly to do with the subordination of the Guatemalan culture and economy to the greater power of the United States of America.

However, a US child wearing Guatemalan cultural artifacts would be responding to a much different set of social relations. The meaning that the US child could attribute to their Guatemalan marker could be exoticism, primitivism, or political solidarity, all of which point to a very different relation of power than what the Guatemalan child is facing.

The general argument of globalization is that these non-local connections are increasing everywhere (for the Guatemalan child and for the child in the US). How these connections shift the structure, tenor, and qualities of cultures is the central theme of this book. If non-local connections are increasing, it becomes important to begin to map our own connections and understand in what ways these connections are social relations and how power works (whether it's a question about buying a pair of Nike sneakers made in Asia or a tourist trip to Cabo San Lucas). But to put this process within a framework, we need to consider briefly how globalization itself has been talked about and present a few models that might help us decide how we should understand our own cultural processes and those of people around us.

Globalization

A first distinction that needs to be made is between the global and the international. The latter is simply that, inter-nations. It discusses the relation of culture, economics, and politics within the framework of the nation-state, a particular organization of government. What makes the term globalization different is that it discusses much more than relations between states, and in fact the state may not always be an actor in the relations that make up the global (see, e.g., Sklair, 1999).

Transnational corporations may by-pass state regulations; some relations are within nations, or have routes through many nations. The term international tends to lock us in to looking at the issue on a particular scale, the scale of the nation-state (American, French, Vietnamese, Sudanese), but many of the changes that globalization purports to address come at many different scales, from the most local (a Korean grocer on that corner in that town) to the most extra-national (global warming knows no borders).

What makes the idea of globalization unique isn't the sets of intricate interconnections between peoples and places, or even the movement of goods around the world. Trade routes stretched the length of the Americas and crossed oceans long before Columbus encountered the West Indies. And global trade today isn't much greater than what it was a century ago (Hirst and Thompson, 1996). What makes globalization new is a sense of the world as a whole; that is, that not only is one aware of other people and places, but there is a sense of simultaneity and interconnection, that events and decisions made in far-off places can have consequences for your everyday life, and that your everyday life can have consequences for many others a world away. Ronald Robertson (1992, p. 8) defined the concept of globalization as referring "both to the compression of the world and the intensification of consciousness of the world as a whole." Is there more to globalization than this sense? Most certainly. There is an extensive literature out there on the topic.[2] But I wish to start with just these ideas.

Let me present two different views on globalization: One more sanguine, one more dire. The more cheery of the two is courtesy of a special issue of *National Geographic* magazine from August 1999; it is one of a number of special issues designed to mark the change of the millennium. In this case, it is an issue about Global Culture. Accompanied by striking photographs, the central article of the issue by Erla Zwingle proclaims in its title: "Goods move. People move. Ideas move. And cultures change." The descriptions that follow in the article present a dizzying array of cosmopolitan culture clashes, constellations of cultural hybridity and cross-cultural consumption. For example: "[H]anging around a pub in New Delhi that serves Lebanese cuisine to the music of a Filipino band in rooms decorated with barrels of Irish stout, a stuffed hippo head, and a vintage poster announcing the Grand Ole Opry concert to be given at the high school in Douglas, Georgia" (p. 12).

The article emphasizes the benefits of globalization: the expansion of modern technologies, the connections and communication between cultures, the increase in choice for consumers, the spread of democracy and human rights, the chance for a better quality of life for many of the world's peoples. As the editor's introduction to the Zwingle article puts it, "Far from uniform, the new global culture is a shifting mixture of experimentation and innovation in which more and less developed societies learn and benefit from one another" (Swerdlow, 1999, p. 4).

What the magazine ignores is the question of power; whether or not this relationship between more- and less-developed societies is a relationship between equals. In many ways, the issue describes the ways that everybody benefits from globalization. It is based on the myth of the global market as a level playing field, that the confrontation between two cultures, say Borneo and the US, would be on an equal footing.

Let me then quickly sketch out the more negative view of globalization. It comes from a book originally published in 1971 entitled, *How to Read Donald Duck: Imperialist Ideology in the Disney Comic.* But first some background. In 1970 Salvador Allende, a Marxist, was elected President of Chile in a free and open election. One of Chile's main resources was copper, and yet most of the national copper industries were actually owned by foreigners, especially Americans. So the country saw little of the profits. One of the actions that Allende took was to nationalize the copper industry. This sort of move, plus the simple fact of a Marxist being leader of a country in its own hemisphere, upset the US government. In a reaction to Allende's election, the US began an unofficial boycott of Chile. Very few American goods were allowed to be shipped to the country. Some of the few things that were allowed in were comic books, especially Disney comics. Ariel Dorfman and Armand Mattelart, two Marxist scholars working in Chile, argued that the comics were not as innocent as they seemed, and their shipment into Chile could be seen as an attempt to undermine the Chilean government through a form of psychological warfare. In 1973 Allende died in a military coup that was supported by the CIA. He was replaced by General Auguste Pinochet, who reprivatized industry and reopened trade with the US. Pinochet's regime, which lasted 17 years, was notorious for its repression, torture, and the murder of dissidents. The book, *How to Read Donald Duck*, was banned and burned in Chile and its authors driven into exile.

So why were comic books considered so dangerous? And what does this have to do with globalization? Dorfman and Mattelart's basic argument was a simple one: any text shares the assumptions and values of the culture within which it was created. A book created in a capitalist society would be assumed to have capitalist values; its setting and the actions its characters took would be in keeping with the norms and assumptions of that society (they would hold certain jobs, and value certain things); a book created in a socialist society would be assumed to have socialist values; and so on. So why is this significant? It is significant because Dorfman and Mattelart noted that there is one genre of literature for which we make an exception to this rule: children's literature, including comic books. Children's literature, we believe, is special; it should create a world of play and fantasy. Children should not be troubled by social ills such as crime, poverty, illness, and the rest. Childhood is a special time held apart from all that. In short, people go out of their way to argue that children's literature is not in any way ideological (and anyone who says that it is must hate children and want to spoil their lives) and that it should be immune to ideology critique. Therefore comic books, especially those by Disney (seen as a child's best friend), are innocent and pure and there is no problem if Chilean adults allow their children to read them. But Dorfman and Mattelart argue that this is nonsense. Comic books are written by particular people in a particular context and therefore the stories, settings, and characters will embody aspects of that context.

So Dorfman and Mattelart set out to describe the world that the Disney comics depict, the characters that one finds there, the sorts of things that go on, and so on, to get a better sense of what values might actually be found in the comics. Their analysis shows that rather than being completely devoid of social issues, the comics bring up third world debt (and the World Bank), Marxist revolutionaries, pollution, crime, gender stereotypes, the exploitation of the third world by the first, and many other social issues. So they ask two critical questions: who or what is missing from the view of the world set out in the Disney comics? And, who benefits if we see the world in this way? In answer to the first question, what is missing in the comics is production of any sort: there is no reproduction (indeed, there are no families, there are only uncles and nephews, aunts and nieces; there is only one parent and child depicted in the comics) and there is no production, meaning that there are no factories, no workers. Indeed, there is no work; work is an adventure that Donald and his friends go on; the treasure that they find is never actually owned by anyone. Who benefits if we see the world this way? In other words, whose view of the world is this? The bourgeoisie, answer Dorfman and Mattelart: a world of stuff to buy, in which jobs are plentiful but not necessary, in which work is an adventure, where one is the rightful owner of treasure simply by being civilized, and in which that pesky working class (always complaining and threatening to start revolutions) is simply absent. The world depicted in the Disney comics, they argue, is a world without love, where nephews and uncles compete with each other for advantage; it is a world where women simply (and only) flirt with men (the eternal girlfriends – Minnie and Daisy) or rise up as evil witches to be defeated. It is a world of stereotypes of masculine and feminine behavior, and cultural stereotypes of all sorts (lazy Mexicans, revolutionary Asians, tribal Africans, and so on).

In addition to these stereotypes, and the general skewed world presented, there is one more aspect from Dorfman and Mattelart's analysis to bring up here. Throughout most of the comics, the adventures involve the heroes traveling to primitive third world countries and either rescuing the natives or cheating the natives in some way (by trading them playful soap bubbles for gold and jewels that the natives don't seem to need). In comic after comic the natives are portrayed as innocent children who need the leadership of the civilized Ducks. The natives have things that are no use to them (old treasure, for example), which the Ducks cheerfully relieve them of. It isn't stealing, since it is given up willingly. This relation between the civilized Ducks and the natives parallels the relation between the industrialized West and the third world (who are seen to be primitive innocents without means to really use all that oil or all those minerals, and besides who would want to spoil their innocent bliss by actually letting them in on the secret of industry and wealth?). This exploitative relationship, Dorfman and Mattelart argue, is a form of imperialism. The comics themselves, when distributed worldwide, are also a form of imperialism, cultural imperialism. They carry with them the values of the society in which they were created. The children who read those comics, and who then act out these adventures in their play, begin to take on the values of the comics (to focus on oneself before others, that relationships are about competition, that one should continually buy things, and that it is only those from the big cities who have all the right knowledge and ideas about how to do things.) This, they argue, is an imperialism of the children's minds and of the culture that the children grow up in. This is not the equal exchange of ideas indicated by the *National Geographic*. This sees these connections of culture and home-making as potentially exploitative and imperialistic. Where the *National Geographic* ignored the question of power in these relations, in *How to Read Donald Duck*, there is nothing but power.

Dorfman and Mattelart's study is a classic in many ways: it is a close and careful Marxist reading of a popular text (well documented and profusely illustrated, arguments are usually carefully supported) and it clearly spells out how when culture moves it doesn't always result in happy hybridity. Now let me be clear, Dorfman and Mattelart have nothing against the Disney comics themselves. They are not arguing that they should not exist (at least, they are not arguing so in this particular book). Rather they are arguing that they may be inappropriate for the cultural and economic context of Chile at that time: given the fragile economy, telling citizens not to work together but only to look out for themselves and to buy things that they cannot afford is self-destructive.

What we need to take from this extended example of *How to Read Donald Duck* is the notion of cultural imperialism, which I will expand upon below. But first we need to note some very real issues with Dorfman and Mattelart's analysis. The main problem is this: the authors only address the things that they see in the texts, and they assume that what is in the text is taken up directly by the reader (though not directly in a conscious way; the things seen in the texts influence the readers on an ideological level; on the general level of assumptions). They do not see, for example, that a reader of the comics might read them in a very different way and incorporate them into a quite different ideology, and that children may indeed play at being Donald

Duck, but how that play occurs and what meanings these children take from it is not addressed. This is the question of reception and it is an important one which we will return to, but it is also important not to overemphasize.

Before moving on to discuss the idea of cultural imperialism and other approaches to globalization, I would like to take this opportunity to apply Dorfman and Mattelart's key critical questions to the *National Geographic* article: who is missing from this view of the world? And who benefits if we see the world this way? The answers are surprisingly similar to Dorfman and Mattelart's (though the magazine is not talking about uncles and parents). Who is missing is the working class. In its sojourns across the new globalized world, in its interviews with slum dwellers and entrepreneurs, the magazine consistently ignores the working class and indeed the entire aspect of production. In a world of amazing diverse goods, in a global supermarket of culture, Dorfman and Mattelart might ask, who is making all this stuff? Maquiladoras on the US/Mexico border, sweatshops in New York and Hong Kong, sweltering factories in Southeast Asia and Central America are all part of globalization too, but surprisingly silent, absent from the richly evocative photographs that the magazine is known for. Who benefits? Zwingle's article states it quite clearly: one of the benefits of globalization is that exports from California and Idaho have risen 200–300 percent (Zwingle, 1999, pp. 32–3). To see globalization as purely a world of consumption and not production ignores the very real everyday lives of those who have to make this stuff in conditions that are appalling.[3]

Global Flows

What has been called the cultural imperialism thesis has been powerfully persuasive in early theories of globalization. Cultural imperialism argues that while the old political empires have crumbled, the Western nations still control the symbolic and cultural world by controlling the mass media. Though foreign troops may not be deployed, and a foreign government established, the presence of the empire is felt in the everyday presence of Western media products. It is not just third world countries that are feeling defensive against this cultural threat:

Europe has felt it as well. For decades there have been ongoing debates in Europe (and the UK) about encroaching Americanization. Many countries establish import quotas on American media goods, and require that their television and radio stations play a certain percentage of local content. The country that has the world's attention as a warning of what might happen is Canada. Located along an open border with the US, and lacking a language difference (except in Quebec) that could insulate the country from US media, the Canadian media system is swamped with US content. Most films shown, television shows viewed, CDs or magazines purchased, or music aired are from the US. Plus most of the Canadian population lives close enough to the US border to simply tune in to US broadcasts. Canadian government regulations have struggled to support and subsidize Canadian content that espouses Canadian values (Dorland, 1996). The Europeans worry that they might all "become Canadians" (Perlmutter, 1993).

The problem with the cultural imperialism thesis is that it assumes that the process of globalization is a one way flow: from the West (read: America) to the rest. Especially in the 1970s, media scholarship supported this view, giving evidence of how the West dominated the global film and television industries as well as the international news services such as the Associated Press and Reuters. The cultural imperialism thesis also assumes that this process is uniform and occurs in the same way everywhere. That is, it assumes that the world will become homogenized, that it will look the same wherever you go. And one can find numerous examples of this: international tourist hotels look much the same worldwide, the same fast food restaurants are available, the same television channels are on (CNN, MTV), and so on. It assumes that the American media will have the same effect on Indonesia as it does on New Zealand or Egypt. Basically, the cultural imperialism thesis contains the same flaw as Dorfman and Mattelart's argument: it doesn't consider the process of reception. But it also ignores competing processes of cultural movement. Perhaps there isn't just one global flow of information and entertainment, but multiple flows?

Political scientist Benjamin Barber, in an influential yet problematic book entitled *Jihad v. McWorld*, argues that globalization actually consists of two different processes working in opposite directions. One of these processes he names McWorld. This is the steady homogenization of the world by the giant transnational corporations. The world becomes a single market and McDonald's, Marriotts, MGM films, and Microsoft are everywhere. But there is an opposite process at work which he terms Jihad, the resistance against this coming McWorld. Jihad, a term he borrows loosely from Islam, refers to a conservative, traditional backlash against the encroaching Westernization. It refers to groups clinging more fiercely (and indeed blindly) to what they see as their core beliefs. We can see this in the rise of religious fundamentalism among both Christians and Muslims, and in the terrorist attacks on the US and its allies. Each process, he argues, has its benefits: McWorld does increase choice for many people and can raise standards of living; Jihad can provide one a sense of identity, of belonging to a group, which is often lacking in the modern world. But each has its disadvantages as well: McWorld can be destructive of other forms of culture and thought and it reduces the world into things to be bought; Jihad can be stifling, hierarchical, and lack many freedoms. Neither option, Barber points out, is democratic. Consumer choice is not the same as political choice and traditional groups are not run freely and openly. One problem here is that the situation is described too simply. This binary reinforces the Orientalist notion that Islam is anti-modern and anti-Western.

Globalization is a much more complex process than any simple binary can describe. We cannot just discuss opposing forces, as if each were that uniform and that these were our only choices. Barber's globalization schema assumes that global flows are much more regular and coordinated than they are. That global flows are anything but coordinated or regular is an insight that we owe to anthropologist Arjun Appadurai (1996) who, in a very influential essay, argued that we can't think of globalization as a single dimension. There are actually multiple dimensions to globalization and these different dimensions at times contradict each other and combine in unpredictable ways. Appadurai asks us to consider the world in terms of a map or landscape. If we look at the world according to economics, then we get one particular map with key financial centers marked and important flows of investment and information connecting specific places. But if we look at the world according to the movement of peoples we get a different topography; we see people moving to where jobs are, or away from famines or wars, or towards the latest trendy tourist hotspot. Each of these dimensions he refers to as a "scape" (short for landscape). And he delineates five such scapes:

- *ethnoscape*: the landscape of persons; tourists, immigrants, refugees, exiles, guest workers;
- *technoscape*: the landscape of technology and the distribution of technologies globally; this includes to where manufacturing plants move;
- *finanscape*: the landscape of money and investment; this includes stock exchanges, monetary exchanges, loans, and investments (follow the money!);
- *mediascape*: the landscape of images and stories; and
- *ideoscape*: the landscape of political ideas (such as freedom, democracy and social justice).

Each of these landscapes moves in a slightly different way and each movement has implications for the others. The movement of a group of guest workers from a home country to another country for employment has economic effects on both countries. This group also brings with them their own media images (and the desire to import more media images from their home culture) and cuisine and political ideas. The resulting economic changes might have implications for global money markets and potential investment in either country by the World Bank or others.

Global flows, Appadurai argues, occur in and through the disjunctures between the scapes. Adding to this image of global turbulence – as opposed to global conformity – philosophers Gilles Deleuze and Félix Guattari (1987, p. 468) have argued that there are four flows that will most "torment the representatives of the world economy": matter-energy (which Appadurai doesn't consider since he's focusing on the cultural dimensions of globalization and not the physical), population, food, and the urban flow. In any case, all these flows cause a global turbulence such that global homogenization is all but impossible (Malcolm Waters (1995) refers to this as the New World Chaos).[4] Since globalization relies on all these dimensions it is doubtful that any one culture or country can dominate all of them (and control all the flows of people, money, images, and so on).

But just because global homogenization is impossible, that the global is chaotic, and that domination of all flows simultaneously is difficult, this does not imply that we should hop on board the happy hybridity bandwagon with *National Geographic*. All these scapes are structured by power relations and both historical and contemporary networks and institutions of economic, political, and military imperialism. Though the overt empires based in Europe are gone, this does not mean that the imperial centers of Europe and North America have little influence, or equal influence with other nations, on world affairs.[5] The US, especially and predominantly these days, is an imperial power whether Americans think of themselves in these terms or not.

What is key for Appadurai's overall argument is the idea of imagined community, which he borrows from Benedict Anderson (1983). The basic idea is this: we live with a sense of community with others. Whereas once this community was of those we knew face to face, with communication technologies from the printing press on, we feel we are part of a community with those far away from us, people whom we may never meet. Anderson uses the term to explain the rise of the idea of the nation: that there is a greater community that one is a part of and which one feels such loyalty towards that one deeply identifies with it (I am French, American, Russian . . .) to the extent that one would go to war over it. Appadurai broadens its use a bit to think of all those non-local connections that make up who we feel we are. With the increased movement of people (ethnoscape) and images (mediascape) people's imagined communities (and, therefore, the resources that they draw on in their own processes of home-making) are getting more complex, are becoming global, and aren't necessarily tied to a particular plot of land. Appadurai (1996, p. 4) provides examples:

> As Turkish guest workers in Germany watch Turkish films in their German flats, as Koreans in Philadelphia watch the 1988 Olympics in Seoul through satellite feeds from Korea, and as Pakistani cabdrivers in Chicago listen to cassettes of sermons recorded in mosques in Pakistan or Iran, we see moving images meet deterritorialized viewers. These create diasporic public spheres, phenomena that confound theories that depend on the continued salience of the nation-state as the key arbiter of important social changes.

In the midst of all of these movements, Appadurai asks, how do cultures reproduce themselves? A family, for example, can't assume stability in the passage of knowledge from generation to generation as members (and entire generations) of the family move to other countries, marriages are strained as are traditions that conflict with the culture of a new country. People lose the firm cultural landmarks of their traditions and culture becomes less a habitus and more conscious because one has to work to maintain one's connections (p. 44). The media provide powerful resources that allow people to territorialize and maintain some sense of identity, but which can also be used (especially by youth) to rebel against their parents (p. 45).

There is another way of critiquing the singular flow of the cultural imperialism thesis and that is pointing out the multiple directions of flows. The classic cultural imperialism thesis argues that the culture is produced in the West (usually California) and is then distributed around the globe. Tamar Liebes and Elihu Katz (1990, p. v) put it this way: "Theorists of cultural imperialism assume that hegemony is prepackaged in Los Angeles, shipped out to the global village, and unwrapped in innocent minds." But if we look closely at the global flows, we can discern regional flows. For example, within South America the center of media production isn't the US but Brazil, whose TV Globo produces telenovelas and programs that are then translated from Portuguese into Spanish and redistributed throughout Central and South America. Globo programs have also proved popular in Portugal, reversing the old colonial flow of influence (see, e.g., Mader, 1993; Sinclair, 1996). If we look to Asia we see that India produces more films per year than any other country in the world and that the production of Hindi films in Bombay (referred to as Bollywood films) dominate the Indian market. In fact, these films are exported around the world to countries with substantial Indian populations (the result of colonialism as well as the search for job opportunities), but also to countries that find the films' cultural values and aesthetics comport well with their own. In July, 2003, an Indian musical debuting in the US had the sixteenth highest grosses of the week in the US market and made more money per screen than the big Hollywood blockbuster of that week (*Entertainment Weekly*, July 11, 2003). Further East, we can find Hong Kong as a key source of films for the diasporic Chinese community, and in terms of popular culture many in Southeast Asia worry more about the dominance of Japan than the US.

Over the past few years, however, the very direction of even these regional flows has been questioned. Let me give you an example from Yoshiko Nakano (2002). The late 1990s saw an interesting invasion of Hong Kong. Everywhere one went one saw references to the latest Japanese television drama series. The shows were amazingly popular. If one wasn't up on the latest series, one was out of the social loop. The strange thing was, these different series (J-dramas, as they are called) were not being broadcast on television and were not available on any cable or satellite channel. They were all pirated on VCDs (Video Compact Disks, like DVDs but more readily playable on computers as well as TVs).[6] In computer labs, people could be seen hunched over their computers watching episode after episode on their computer's CD-ROM drive. The pirated VCDs even infiltrated into mainland China itself. What is interesting about this phenomenon is that this surge in popularity for Japanese cultural products occurred without the Japanese being aware of it, especially the Japanese producers of these series. Indeed, they were quite surprised by the news. So while on the surface this example could be of the cultural imperialism of Japan in Asia, pushing its culture onto neighboring countries, the exact opposite is the case. This is a case of *pull*, which complicates the picture of cultural globalization. Indeed these exchanges of cultural products within Southeast Asia, both formal and informal (that is, illegal) have created a new public sphere of popular culture where products from a variety of countries get pulled (and pushed) into new markets depending on the desires of consumers. This new public sphere is not centered on one hub (unless that hub is Hong Kong, which acts as a distributor, but not a monitor, for the region).

This was not the first time Japanese popular culture has seen success in Hong Kong. There is a long history of popularity of Japanese products in Hong Kong, from comics[7] to TV shows to pop music. And the importation of some of these products was also a form of pull rather than push. As the Hong Kong television industry was getting on its feet in the late 1960s and early 1970s, dubbed Japanese programs helped fill airtime. And as Masashi Ogawa (2001, 2004) has noted, the Hong Kong music industry in the 1980s would import

Japanese pop songs and produce local cover versions to make up for the lack of strong Hong Kong-based songwriters.

The why's and where's of the pull and push of cultural texts vary from place to place, group to group. For example, J-dramas are attractive to audiences because they have high production values and attractive casts, and tend to be well written. Once they become popular they become the topic of conversation and media coverage and people have to watch them just to be a part of these conversations (Nakano, 2002). In Hong Kong, which was incorporated back into mainland China in 1997 after a long period of British rule, the consumption of Japanese products might be a statement of independence from the PRC (People's Republic of China) – Hong Kong citizens identify much more with the sophisticated cosmopolitanism of Japan than what they consider the provincialism of China.

In Taiwan, Japanese products have also become very popular, especially after a long-term ban on broadcasts of Japanese content in Taiwan was lifted in 1993. The reason for the attraction in Taiwan varies by generation. Japan had occupied Taiwan for 50 years until the end of World War II, and so there are traces of Japanese cultural influence within Taiwanese cultural life (Iwabuchi, 2005). Older generations of Taiwanese still speak Japanese and many have a lingering nostalgia for the Japanese culture of their youth. But for young audiences the attraction is that they can relate to the situations of the urban Japanese characters. Iwabuchi (2005, p. 23) writes that "one of the attractions of Japanese TV drama is its new style of portraying love, work, and women's position in society." Young audiences in Taiwan just didn't see portrayals like this, which they found somewhat realistic and relatable, in domestic Taiwanese drama or imported American dramas.[8]

The cultural imperialism thesis is premised on a model of center and periphery – the imperial center dominates the periphery and the periphery looks to the center with desire. We'll talk more about this relationship as the book progresses. But I want to note here that this discussion of the flow of J-dramas has little to do directly with a Western or American-dominated imperialism. And it is not the case that Japan has simply become another imperial center. Indeed, Japan has been reluctant to push its products in Asia – though they sell very well – because of its own imperial history (and Korea and Taiwan had banned its products for decades because of their histories as Japanese colonies) but also because its own domestic market is so strong that it doesn't need the foreign revenue as much, as well as other reasons (Iwabuchi, 2001; Nakano, 2002). The Taiwanese youth don't watch J-dramas because they yearn to be Japanese or to experience Japanese modernity, but because they recognize in these dramas a lived reality similar to their own Taiwanese modernity (Iwabuchi, 2005), a reality not found represented in other cultural products.

By 2001 J-dramas were becoming passé in Hong Kong, and the latest rage were K-dramas (Korean dramatic TV series) and even K-pop (Korean popular music). This was known as the "Korean Wave." Iwabuchi (2005, p. 33) notes that "Taiwanese viewers now perceive Korean TV dramas, which subtly depict youth's love affairs in connection with family matters, as 'ours' even more than Japanese TV dramas." One reason for this is that the Korean dramas include family relationships more than Japanese dramas do (Iwabuchi, 2004). In fact, Korean dramas and music were even becoming popular in Japan. By the time this book sees print, who knows what the latest trend will be? To understand the cultural exchanges in Southeast Asia (as a microcosm of globalization) we need a much more flexible and nuanced model of what is happening.

Form and Content, Local and Global

Local form/global content

Let's take up the issue of reception once again. Tamar Liebes and Elihu Katz conceived a research study in the 1980s to begin to understand the global popularity of the American television show *Dallas* (Liebes and Katz, 1990). Why was it so popular? Was this simply cultural imperialism? What sense did diverse audiences make of the show, and did all audiences get the same meanings from watching the show? What Katz and Liebes argued, through a comparative cross-cultural study, was that audiences interpreted (or decoded) the series through their own experiences and cultural frameworks. For example, they would see the show as confirming (or denying, which in some ways is confirming by negative example) the audience's traditional values (perhaps filial loyalty), or try to attribute motivations to the characters perhaps at odds with the particular story at hand but which fit the audience's frame of reference. The meanings of the show, in other words, would get repackaged from within the framework of the audience's local culture.

Global content (content distributed globally) is given a local form through the interpretations and discussions of the audiences that consume it. In a similar way (remember our discussion of popular culture in the last chapter) global culture can be appropriated for local uses, to make a local statement about identity. Richard Wilk (1995) reports, for example, that during Belize's struggle for independence from Britain the opposition would fly US flags not necessarily out of loyalty to the US (and everything that it stands for) but because it meant "not British." Local news reports in many regions may literally bring the global content within a local form by rebroadcasting (and at times reediting) footage from foreign news sources (including CNN) but often talking over the English of the original's soundtrack to present the story within a local ideological framework. To be fair, the US media often do the same thing. It can be an interesting exercise to decipher the competing news logo "burn-ins" on the screen (NBC over ITV over Xinhua . . .).

This process of localization is not unknown to the global corporations who will take a global product (McDonald's hamburgers, Revlon cosmetics) and produce local versions of it (McMutton sandwiches, make-up with the color palette suited to South Asian faces, and so on (see Zwingle, 1999)).

Global form/local content

Anthropologist Richard Wilk (1995) argues that the nature of globalization, of global capitalism, and, therefore, of global cultural hegemony, has changed. Global capitalism no longer promotes homogeneity, it is not trying to mass produce one widget for the entire world. That old strategy can be opposed, by those so inclined, by arguing in favor of cultural difference (we're different and so your widget won't work here, go home). What global capitalism does today is that it actually promotes difference (the new, the exotic), and it thrives on difference. But it promotes only a certain type of difference, and ignores other differences. It promotes the types of differences that can be easily packaged and sold, the types of differences that are not threatening to global capitalism. By promoting a limited range of difference, it limits the range of actions available to people. Wilk refers to this as *structures of common difference*, an apparently paradoxical statement.

What does he mean by structures? Wilk gives the example of staying up late at night watching television and becoming fascinated with the American Double-Dutch League Jump-Rope Championships. Jump rope, presumably a creative childhood game or activity, had become professionalized and commodified. There were teams, with sponsors, and there were judges and events. The whole event was presented within the same framework usually given over to professional sports (including commentators and interviews and slow motion replays). But what does it mean to professionalize jump rope? What it means is that the previously chaotic and creative activity of jump rope had been standardized and structured. In order to have a competition there must be a comparison, standards and a scoring system. There is then a right and wrong way to perform jump rope moves (which have become delineated and named). Some aspects of the activity had been highlighted (some moves were chosen as standards for the repertoire that everyone would perform for the competition) and others had been ignored. In terms of the competitors themselves, some differences were made to matter (teams and individuals competed by age) and others were ostensibly ignored (teams were not segregated by gender or race, at least not by the rules – they tended to be segregated based on the gender coding of jump rope as a girl's activity and racially by the socioeconomics of the team's home town such as inner city or suburb). By structuring this free play, jump rope becomes intelligible nationally and globally. Jump rope is placed within the global form of professionalized sports (with records, rules, standards, skills) which is intelligible if one understands that form. In order to understand, at least in a general way, what is going on in any number of sports, knowing the global form allows one to figure some of it out. For example, sitting in a hotel room in Seoul, Korea, one night, I ended up watching a Sumo wrestling match from Japan on the television. I hadn't a clue what was going on, but I could understand that there was scoring (by the box scores superimposed on the bottom of the screen) and who was ahead, and by the tone of the commentators what was considered a significant occurrence or not. This structure allows Sumo matches to occur around the globe, if they wished, and for the matches to be comparable at some level, just as the structuring of jump rope allows global jump rope competitions to occur. But I would argue that jump rope loses something in the transition, just as the local idiosyncrasies of a Sumo match are lost in the lists of statistics. Jump rope is not alone in this structuring; other creative activities have become standardized so that they can become competitions, so that they can travel: marching bands, ballroom dance, canoeing, cheerleading, water ballet.

By imposing a common structure on activities, difference can be controlled. One can be different, but only according to the rules. All these various "sports" are different, but they share a common set of differences; it is a structure of common difference. In terms of global capital and culture, a similar process is in place according to Wilk. Cultures are allowed to be different (and indeed capitalism will promote these differences to the nth degree), but only in certain, marketable, safe ways. What differences are cultures allowed to have in the global arena? Language, food, dance, arts, religion, and ethnicity (one's looks) are all usually safe. Indeed, if one is a tourist one looks for the local cuisine, arts, rituals and festivals, and enjoys watching the exotic people. What differences are cultures *not* allowed to have in the global arena? Politics and economics (non-capitalist value systems), and extreme religious beliefs. These tend to dampen tourism and global trade. Tales of globalization that praise the idea of the global supermarket tend to focus on the former differences and ignore the latter (we saw this in the example of the *National Geographic* issue). Be as different as you want, but only in certain well-defined ways that won't rock the boat. Wilk gives the example of an indigenous tribe in Belize, which was in an uprising over land rights (an unacceptable form of difference); in response the Belizean government supplied them with videocameras so that they could record their local dances and rituals (an acceptable form of difference). Wilk's main example, too extensive to get into here, is the use of beauty pageants in Belize as a platform for politics, where local differences in culture, aesthetics, and politics are exhibited (and compete) through a series of local, regional, and national contests.

Proponents of cultural imperialism used to focus solely on the presence of foreign content in local contexts (how many US films were on Thai screens, how many hours of Peruvian television were taken up with US programming, and so on). But Wilk raises the interesting question, what if the content is local but it is expressed in a foreign (or "global") form? This same concern has been raised by those studying global television. Concern moved from the presence of *Dallas* on foreign TV screens to the presence of locally produced *Dallas* knock-offs on foreign TV screens. Could the form itself be ideological? The answer is yes, by focusing on some aspects of a situation but not others. For example, the soap opera focuses on interpersonal relations and conflict; it presents a particular way of looking at the world whether the actors are French or American. Game shows would be an easier example; they promote particular types of competition, for wealth and prizes, and not cooperation. And so on.

Susan Davis (1996) raises an interesting example of global form and local content in her discussion of global theme parks. Much ink has been spilled about the particular ideologies of the various Disneylands, but what Davis is interested in is whether the form of the corporate-sponsored theme park itself (whether owned by Disney, AOL Time Warner (Six Flags), or Sanrio) could be hegemonic. The theme park, as a global form, is a self-contained, closely controlled leisure space:

> The theme park landscape as it has developed is exhaustively commercial to its core, a virtual maze of advertising, public relations and entertainment, especially in the chain parks. It is the site for the carefully controlled sale of goods (souvenirs) and experiences (architecture, rides and performances) "themed" to the corporate owner's proprietary images. (Davis, 1996, p. 402)

The experience of a theme park space is one that has been carefully planned out; as a visitor you are carefully led to experience the park in a certain way, to engage in certain activities (going on rides, taking pictures, and, most of all, buying things) and not others. The well-run theme park is a machine that teaches people how to relax and have fun, but most of all teaches them how to consume. Visits to theme parks become ritualized (people return again and again, especially on special occasions). Davis cites John Kasson as arguing that Coney Island, the amusement park that was the model for those that followed:

> helped teach the American middle class new habits of relaxation, sociability, and consumption. . . . Undoubtedly, the American-style theme park can be seen as accomplishing the same thing for the newly wealthy in the poorer world. But which patterns of consumption these are, and whether they serve the interests of whole populations, is a subject that needs further investigation. (Davis, 1996, p. 415)

In the variety of local theme parks that Davis describes, popping up all over the world, local themes and products can be emphasized. But these themes and products are presented within the same structure of difference. They may sell different products and use different characters and images, but they all use corporate sponsorship and encourage visitors to consume at every turn. As well, they encourage people to spend their leisure time in certain ways (going to a theme park) and not others (which might be less focused on consumption).

One more example of a global form and local content before we're through: karaoke. I'm discussing karaoke here because we can think of it as a global form that did not originate in the West, but in Japan. Here is a cultural practice that has a generally similar format worldwide (screen with words, music playing without vocals, a microphone, a stage area, and a volunteer to sing) but in which the content is usually fairly local (what songs are sung, what language they're sung in). Karaoke began in Japan in the 1970s as a technological version of the cultural practice of singing in public (especially in bars) accompanied by roving musicians. The technology eliminated the need for the musicians. The practice of karaoke was exported from Japan following the movements of Japanese businessmen; it tended to spring up in bars catering to that clientele. From there it would spread out into the local culture depending on a number of factors: the structure of the entertainment industry in that country, the presence of a local practice of public singing (like singing in pubs in Britain), and the country's image of Japan (Otake and Hosokawa, 1998). The latter factor was especially important to karaoke's spread in Southeast Asian countries which had a long history of Japanese imperialism to be factored in.

As Casey Man Kong Lum (1998) has argued, when we talk about karaoke we need to talk about a karaoke space that is created (the space of performance and audience). Karaoke creates a particular space (or territory) with particular social rules; in this way it is a cultural space as well. The rules of the karaoke space include a subtle and not-so-subtle pressure for everyone to perform and for the audience to be appreciative of the singer's efforts. These rules vary in intensity (and other rules may apply) depending on the specific karaoke space created (whether in a public space like a bar, a private meeting room, or at home in a living room, or the culture of those participating). In some contexts there is an insistence that everyone sing; in other contexts the shy are excused. The space of karaoke is a collective space in some ways, in that there is the collective pressure to participate and to support others (rather than jeering), but it is a collective space in which an individual performance (or occasionally a duo) will be the central focus. This space is then negotiated in different ways by karaoke participants.

Lum provides profiles of three different immigrant Chinese communities in the Northeastern US, each of which negotiates karaoke differently. In Chinatown in New York, Cantonese-speaking Chinese immigrants from Hong Kong "use karaoke as a cultural connection" especially through the singing of songs from Cantonese opera (Lum, 2001, p. 129; see also Lum, 1998). Taiwanese immigrants in New Jersey use karaoke as a means of displaying their affluent social class. And Malaysian Chinese in a working class community in Queens, New York City, utilize karaoke as an escape. Each group tends to use karaoke to express a particular ethnic identity. Though Americans tend to view all Chinese as Chinese, there are substantial ethnic and cultural differences between Hong Kong Chinese, Taiwanese Chinese, Chinese from other Asian countries (like Singapore or Malaysia), and between regions within mainland China itself. This identity is expressed in the relative ethnic and class homogeneity of those participating in a particular karaoke space as well as the sorts of songs sung (Cantopop from Hong Kong, Japanese influenced ballads from Taiwan, Chinese opera, and so on).

We can consider karaoke as a means of territorializing (home-making), but in this process we need to recognize that we territorialize with what is available and negotiate that territorialization with the object's or relation's own territorializations. One sings karaoke in a particular way as part of one's cultural territorialization (or habitus), but karaoke also helps to shape that territorialization. One learns to sing, but in the style of the pop singers. Let's take the example of Dance Video games such as Dance Dance Revolution (DDR), which has been called "karaoke for the feet" (see Smith, J., 2004). DDR is a video game, located in video arcades, in which the player actually performs dance moves on a small dance floor in front of the machine. The machine itself plays the music and scrolls complex notation for foot placement and dance moves. The machine then scores your accuracy and ability to dance and will comment on your performance. Such a performance is similar to karaoke in that it is usually performed before a crowd, but dissimilar in that one's performance is judged and scored. In a way what the DDR presents is the structuring of another creative activity: dance. A Japanese invention, but available worldwide, DDR is an interesting cultural splicing of Japanese aesthetics, American competition, and aspects of Europop (especially reflected in the techno-flavored music). One learns to dance in a particular way; one tailors one's performance to the machine (and not the crowd, though they could spur one on to meet the machine's demands better). Similar types of video games include drum kits (where one taps out an elaborate drum solo following the directives and notation of the machine) and guitars. These are like karaoke in that they are individual performances with prerecorded machines in a public space, but they differ in their more competitive gaming dimension.

This dynamic of local and global is important for understanding how globalization works today, especially consideration of the structures of common difference. Iwabuchi (2002, p. 44) writes:

> [A] convincing analysis of the unevenness of global interconnectedness should go beyond a global–local binary opposition. The operation of global cultural power can only be found in local practice, whereas cultural reworking and appropriation at the local level necessarily takes place within the matrix of global homogenizing forces.

For many in East Asia, what they share is the common experience of indigenizing Western culture and modernity. What this has produced is a myriad of local modernities, not a uniform modernity and certainly not any straightforward Westernization or Americanization.

> [P]referred cultural products in the region are not without east Asian flavor, as those are reworked in Asian context by hybridizing various latest fads [from] all over the world; they are inescapably global and (East) Asian at the same time, lucidly representing intertwined composition of global homogenization and heterogenization in east Asian context. (Iwabuchi, 2005, p. 20)

Audiences tend to prefer content that they can relate to. The term used is that audiences prefer content that is *culturally proximate* to their own culture and experience (Iwabuchi, 2005; Sinclair et al., 1996; Straubhaar, 1991). But Iwabuchi cautions us not to essentialize the cultural in cultural proximity, that is not to assume that there are some core "Asian values" that East Asian countries share, and that is why they now prefer each other's products over American ones (which tend to be more culturally distant). Rather, cultural proximity is based on a number of factors including common experiences, such as the common experience of dealing with forced modernization through the introduction of Western cultural products (not to mention the history of Western economic, political, and military imperialism in the region, and so on). Remember that Taiwanese audiences liked J-dramas and K-dramas better than American dramas not because of some shared notion of essentialized Asianness, but because they represented a familiar experience of negotiating romantic, family, and social relationships in a particular context of urban modernity. They looked to Japan not as a dream of what life might be like someday, but for practical advice from a country they see as a contemporary of their own. This does not mean that they ignore differences between Taiwan and Japan or that they see the Japanese as the same culturally as the Taiwanese, but that they see them as culturally proximate.

We've been talking about how East Asian countries consume Japanese cultural products as an example of regional cultural flows. But to complicate this view of cultural flow further we need to ask, as Koichi Iwabuchi does, if Japan consumes cultural products from East Asia, and how. The imbalance of flows, and the direction of those flows, is an important dimension to globalization. For example, while most of the world is exposed to American cultural products, the domestic American market remains fairly insular, relatively few foreign texts make it into the US media. Back to the discussion of East Asia. Traditionally, Japan has not consumed a lot of products from the rest of Asia in part because Japan usually views the rest of the region as premodern and primitive and itself as exceptional and modern. With the Asian economic boom and the rapid modernization of many parts of East Asia over the past couple of decades, Singapore, Korea, Taiwan, and Hong Kong in particular are closing the economic gap with Japan, though it is still hard for the Japanese to perceive them as equals or even contemporaries. Recently Japan has begun to consume cultural products from the region – especially films and music from Hong Kong and music and TV dramas from Korea. But, as Iwabuchi (2002, 2005) has argued, they consume them nostalgically, as products of an old Asia which doesn't share Japan's troubles and still has a cultural vigor and optimism which Japan has lost. Or they consume them as examples of a contemporary society, but one which has negotiated modernity differently than Japan has (retaining its cultural vigor and optimism). This latter attitude still leaves in place Japan's general attitude about Asia as something from Japan's primitive past (Iwabuchi, 2002).

The cultural flows in East Asia are particular and uneven, but they are also inextricable from the global flow of cultural products, predominantly Western, which they rework and repurpose. We began this chapter with a consideration of non-local connections in culture-making and how these connections, articulations, and relations are not innocent and voluntary, but imbued with power relations, territorialized by global processes of economics, and the movements of peoples, monies, images, and ideas. One needs to ask which objects, images or ideas are available to one in the first place (which spices can be bought at your supermarket, what videos can be rented from the Vietnamese store down the block, what clothing style is currently in fashion and, therefore, on department store shelves, what is heard on the radio, and so on). Each object, image, or idea has a trajectory, a history, and is made available through the negotiation of many of Appadurai's scapes. The increased circulation of cultural texts predominantly concerns particular urban centers and ignores (both in terms of representations and flows) the non-urban. Entire countries are off the global cultural radar, their images and products absent from the global flow (Iwabuchi, 2005). Which objects, images, or ideas are not available to you and why not? One also needs to question one's own territorializations. How is power being exercised if I start wearing Guatemalan woven bracelets like those discussed in the opening of this chapter? Is this to be "cool" or to express some solidarity with the third world (economic, political, cultural) or to thumb my nose at the dominant culture? Do I see my non-local connections through (as Susan Davis puts it) "imperial eyes"? As colorful ethnic exoticism? The point here is to begin to raise questions about one's own practices. It is not to simply impose guilt on Western readers. Guilt can be as condescending a reaction as exploitative exoticism. Endless hand-wringing about what "we" have done to "them" ignores both the creativity (and collusion) of "them" in the process, and it makes "them" into passive victims. It also essentializes a difference between them and us. But at the same time, showing that local audiences creatively appropriate and indigenize Western goods doesn't erase the sheer economic power of the West, which put its products there and which made them such attractive objects. The point, then, is to begin to understand the specifics of the non-local connections we may draw on to make sense of our daily lives and to construct our senses of ourselves, the concrete historicity of these articulations so that if we choose we may struggle to change them.

Notes

1 On the relation between *roots* and *routes*, see also Paul Gilroy, who argues about "rethinking the dialectical tension between cultural roots and cultural routes" (1992, p. 305) or Iain Chambers' book *Border Dialogues* (1990), or Les Back's (1995) article on Apache Indian which brings Chambers and Gilroy together.

2 For overviews, see, e.g., Ellwood (2001), Featherstone (1990), Hannerz (1996), Robertson (1992), Sklair (1995), Waters (2001). A full overview of globalization would have to include consideration of global economic institutions like the IMF and World Bank, economic policies like the Bretton-Woods agreement and the Washington Consensus, political changes in the nature and power of nation-states, social relations of urbanization, flexible production, modernization and postmodernization,

and so on. For globalization seen in the context of media theory, see the final chapter in Grossberg et al. (2006).

3   The magazine includes a number of striking omissions, or at least rearticulations. Let me provide two examples. There is a striking photograph of a shoeless Black homeless woman sitting in a bus stop in Los Angeles staring at a poster for the film *Armageddon* featuring a glowing close up of actress Liv Tyler's face. The caption for the photograph spends most of its time discussing what an overwhelming global blockbuster the film was and how Hollywood films tend to dominate the film market globally, but apart from simply mentioning the presence of the homeless woman, doesn't discuss how her plight and the plight of the minority urban underclass in the US and elsewhere might be connected to processes of globalization. A second photograph later on features several Indian men playing cards in a slum in Mumbai. Through the entrance to a shack behind them we can see several young women watching television. The caption discusses how India's television has grown from being a government monopoly on a single channel to including hundreds of local and global channels (including MTV and CNN). It does not mention that most of the cable TV systems in India are actually illegal pirate systems (since most cannot afford legitimate systems), and it once again does not mention any possible connection between the conditions that these people are living in and globalization. One could go on. For a more thorough critique of the *National Geographic* issue, see Radhika Parameswaran's 2002 essay, "Local Culture in Global Media: Excavating Colonial and Material Discourses in *National Geographic*," in the journal *Communication Theory*.

4   Waters (1995) adds one more dimension to the cultural scapes: sacriscape, the landscape of religion. He argues that the universalistic religions have been a driving force behind globalization.

5   As Koichi Iwabuchi (2002, p. 48) writes, following Ang and Stratton (1997), "We should not assume that such flows totally replace the old power relations, as the current cultural flows are always already overdetermined by the power relations and geopolitics embedded in the history of imperialism and colonialism."

6   VCDs tend to be a predominantly Asian phenomenon. DVDs utilize copy protection schemes and tend to be popularly associated with the global corporate media industry. VCDs are cheaper and easier to copy, making them more "anarchic" (Hu, 2005).

7   On Japanese comics in Hong Kong, see Lai and Wong (2001).

8   For a comparison of the reception of J-dramas in other East and Southeast Asian countries, see Iwabuchi (2004).

3

Global Youth

As a way of coalescing the previous two chapters on culture and territory and globalization, I want to consider here the case of global youth. I use "global youth" as a term of convenience in that it's somewhat evocative. It's not simply about youth culture or youth culture around the world (like a comparative anthropology of youth) and it's not simply about those who fall into the nebulous category of the young. Global youth is more about youth whose territories have non-local connections. I think this represents a larger percentage of young people around the world than in the past.

But as soon as I raise the term I want to draw back from it nervously and put it at some distance. It is at once too homogeneous and too class-specific a term for my purposes. Global youth often refers to those youth who can afford to travel and consume – raves in Goa, hiking the Andes, and so forth – a particular rarified strata that includes not only affluent Western youth consuming global culture but the children of third-world elites who readily consume high end Western culture. At least, it seems to have these connotations for me. So part of the purpose of this chapter is an attempt to rearticulate this term.

Youth as a Contested Category

Let's start with the idea of youth more broadly because it is a term often invoked unquestioningly. *Youth* as a category is a cultural construction. Any delineation or demarcation of age categories is always culturally and historically specific. When is a child a child and what do we expect children to be able to do or be? Some expect infants to learn independence, some carry infants strapped to their bodies for years. Some send them to factories to work. Some expect them to inhabit a world of innocence and play. When does a child become an adult? Cultures often mark this transition with important rituals – but when these occur and what these transitions mean is tremendously varied even today. "Youth" becomes an even more nebulous category – a space invoked between child and adult, a probationary period (or quarantine) where one becomes an adolescent (literally meaning "becoming adult") or teenager. But, again, what does it mean to be an adolescent or teenager in a culture? What does it mean for the individual teen? What does it mean for society at large? The construction of the idea of *childhood* has been linked to the establishment of formal education in the nineteenth century, and the construction of the idea of *adolescence* originates in the seventeenth century and took hold as capitalism developed. Further education of youth was considered necessary, and more families could afford to provide to their offspring such a space of development. *Teenagers* are often considered an invention of the 1950s and postwar affluence, especially in the US. (For more on all these discussions, see Hebdige (1988) and Valentine et al. (1998).)

All this is generally known. But since these categories seem fixed and have been naturalized, it is sometimes difficult to see them as continually being reinvented – or even invented anew. So let me give you an example of the recent construction of the categories of *youth* and *teenager* in Kathmandu.

Constructing Youth

Anthropologist Mark Liechty (1995, 2003), in his study of the creation of a consumerist middle class culture in Nepal, provides a relevant example of the explicit construction of youth and teen. He relates the example of a new, locally produced in Kathmandu, magazine called, *Teens. Teens* "was conceived of as first and foremost a marketing scheme aimed at upper middle-class youth and designed to move them on to a track leading to membership in the adult consumer club" (Liechty, 1995, p. 172). In this scheme advertisers offer discounts to magazine subscribers, so youth subscribe to get discounts at their favorite stores and restaurants (or, rather, the stores and restaurants which *should* be their favorites, according to the advertisers). The magazine was aimed at English boarding school students because they (or their families) had the affluence the advertisers desired.

> Their aim was to also move into this "in between" space of "teen" ambiguity with a product that would provide youth with answers to questions about what it means to be modern, "to *be* English." From the outset they envisioned a magazine that would provide youth with a blueprint for what it means to be a modern "teen." (Liechty, 1995, pp. 172–3, emphasis in original)

The magazine, therefore, educated youth about youth culture, primarily the commercialized world of media, on the one hand, and a materialistic self-concept on the other. It focused not just on what was hot and popular (usually Western acts and English language songs and videos), but also emphasized personal style – arguing that to be self-conscious about fashion wasn't "shallow" but "hep." In other words, the magazine sold the consumer lifestyle and ideology to local youth. But most importantly for Liechty, the magazine sold the particular idea of the teen. "Its aim is to constitute 'teenage' not so much as an age category, but as a kind of desired condition, a way of life that can be achieved through a range of consumer behaviors" (1995, p. 177). Significantly, the magazine's readership came from across the middle class and not just the initial target group, and across a number of caste and class lines. "Teen" becomes a new identity that these readers were at least intrigued with if not seduced by. The magazine becomes a way of teaching this new group the language of consumerism.

More broadly, Liechty found that the term, "teenager," was used most often by the public to refer to modern, consumerist youth, especially those who consumed drugs, porn, and/or Western media (Liechty, 1995, pp. 179–80). Many, especially adults, used the term "teenager" to refer to delinquent boys and young men. What was happening at that time, Liechty concludes, is a struggle over the meaning of the word, "teenager" – a struggle between those who wanted the term to stand for a modern consumerist lifestyle, and those who saw that lifestyle as corrupting.

The intensity of this struggle over these definitions is certainly not limited to Nepal. Youth are the subject of tremendous cultural investment – seen as the promise of the future, youth are also potentially the means of carrying forward cultural traditions. The apparent seduction of youth by foreign cultural forces is, therefore, perceived as a threat to an entire culture and way of life. However, this way of thinking tends to overly homogenize youth (they're *all* into Western videos and music; they're *all* materialistic consumers, and so on) and view youth as dupes of global capital (as opposed to critical consumers or traditionalists). This cultural investment is also usually gendered: the burden of carrying on a culture falls on the shoulders of girls and women while boys and men are allowed more freedom. Male youth then tend to fall into the category of youth as problem, as delinquent, as a threat, while female youth are what is threatened.

Surveillance and Youth

Both categories of youth, as threat and as threatened, make youth the target of intense social and cultural surveillance. Plus the idea of youth as inherent consumer makes them a target of economic surveillance. On this last point it is estimated that worldwide youth have well over $100 billion in discretionary income and this does not include their influence over their parents or caretaker's spending ("Generation Y," 2003). This is an irresistible market though it is a fickle and cynical one. The time of youth is a time of identity formation, trying out different identities to see who one is or wants to be. Some identities come from parents and cultures around one, others are prepackaged for you and you can buy them and try them on. Youth experiment with identity and equate the use of style as a form of identity (as an expression of self and connection to groups). Note that this falls into the very ideology that Liechty was describing: identity is surface; it's your hairstyle and music choices. Because of this, youth are doubly exploited. On the one hand they are targeted, inundated, and seduced by marketers of global brands. However they tend to be very aware of both these attempts to sell them things (as simply being a way of separating them from their money – that is, they see through the lifestyle rhetoric of the campaigns), and they know what is the product of mainstream marketing and what is actually cool. On the other hand they are exploited as a source of innovation for these very same marketers. So-called cool hunters watch youth for emergent style trends and tastes, the product of youth habitus and territorialization. These attempts by youth to territorialize get packaged and sold back to them and their peers.

The category of youth is a category of suspicion in that youth are often seen as a problem. It seems an acknowledged truth that one of the tasks of youth, especially for boys, is to challenge their traditions (e.g., their fathers) as a means of finding their way and their place in society. However, youth are seen as pushing boundaries too far (they use *too* many drugs, they are *too* promiscuous). And since adolescence is a period when children finish their socialization process, this also means that they are not yet fully socialized (meaning that they are too unstable, impetuous, emotional, and dangerous, having not fully embedded the social within their habits of thought and body – they are not yet responsible citizens). As a result, the study of youth tends to focus around moral panics. A moral panic is a perceived cultural crisis that dictates and focuses public discussion and policy. These tend towards hyperbolic headlines: Youth in Crisis! seems a common focus of moral panic. Gangs! Crime! Sex! Drugs! In the US, research on youth in the 1950s focused on teen gangs and delinquency. Youth were seen as having too much time on their hands, too much leisure, and, amidst post-war affluence, too much money. In the UK, the study of youth was more class-based: the problem was working class youth rather than gangs per se. The justly celebrated cultural studies work on subcultures traced the history of youth as danger. The Teds of the late 1950s were responsible for violent race riots; the Mods of the 1960s projected a certain uncanny style; and the punks of the 1970s rejected core social values (see Hall and Jefferson, 1976; Hebdige, 1979). These groups were studied as *sub*cultures, as reacting to the dominant culture and their parent's culture by poaching cultural artifacts and style and rearticulating them into new cultural formations. Angela McRobbie's work on girls and subcultures (e.g., McRobbie, 2000; McRobbie and Garber, 1976;) acted as a corrective to the male-focused subcultures work, describing girls' territories and practices of identity and cultural formation.

Youth in many ways is not simply an age category but a habitus, a way of being in a territory. Youth territorialize by drawing on different cultures in resistant and nonresistant ways. The Teds appropriated the Edwardian suit, a style created for the British upper classes, and made it their own. The Mods were very careful and critical consumers, highly conscious of style and appearance. And the punks clearly rejected dominant styles, taking the trash and detritus of their society and elevating it to style – trashbags, torn clothing, and so on. But these territories are not just of style or gang turf, but the creation of spaces of their own – youth clubs, bedrooms, restaurants, street corners, parks, malls – amid the spaces controlled by others – school, work, home. In many ways the struggle for territory is an essential part of youth identity. As geographer Doreen Massey (1998, p. 127) has written: "the control of spatiality is part of the process of defining the social category of 'youth' itself." Much of being a youth is determined by where you are allowed to go. Some spaces are reserved for younger children (so, get out of the playground), or older adults (so, get out of the bar). Such rules and restrictions, Massey points out, aren't just about the mobility of youth but their identity and behavior. The social rules that govern spaces govern behavior, and so by regulating the occupancy of space an implicit definition of youth is created and reinforced (they are too old to play like children, but are still corruptible by the adult world). "Even such 'ordinary' rules are bound up with assumptions about identity and attempts to construct socially acceptable identities" (Massey, 1998, p. 127).

The expulsion of the Teds from youth clubs in the 1950s reinforced both the general public representation of the group as violent delinquents (not a "socially acceptable" identity) and the group's own self-identity as outcasts. Their attacks on these same youth clubs could be seen as pure revenge, but also as a defensive move to preserve "a constantly threatened space and a declining status" (Jefferson, 1976, p. 81).

Even today youth don't have to be members of violent gangs (as the Teds were) to be subject to intense social surveillance. For example the relation of youth to public surveillance systems like CCTV is a contentious one. Closed Circuit Television (CCTV) systems are present in most malls and now public spaces, especially in Britain. Youth tend to be closely watched by police and CCTV operators. Being young is one of the categories of suspicion. One CCTV operator in Britain reported that he paid especial attention to suspicious-appearing folks like young men dressed in baggy clothes inspired by hip hop (Smith, J. D., 2004). That he was working on a college campus means that he must have been kept quite busy!

The intensive CCTV surveillance in city centers in Britain is part of an urban renewal process – an attempt to revitalize downtowns by making them safe for shoppers. Ian Toon (2000, p. 151) writes,

> It is the visible presence of youth hanging around on the street that represents a threat to the sense of place, public order and orderliness enforced by the urban regime and this has led to the application of consistent police pressure to limit teenagers' free access to the urban outdoors (particularly at night) by enforcing their eviction from all street, park, wall and bench space in areas under electronic control.

The youth subject to this surveillance are acutely aware of being targeted and why they are targeted. They are constantly moved on even if they are behaving appropriately. Girls in Toon's study are also aware of the gendering of this surveillance: that is, that they are being subject to a male surveillant gaze. But youth do not passively accept this control. Rather they get to know the CCTV system, find places that aren't watched to meet, find paths that are less surveilled through the city centers, find ways of moving on camera that arouse the least suspicion. As one teen put it, "It's like 'hide and seek' now in town with all those cameras" (Toon, 200, p. 154).

Let me give you another example of this struggle for territory and identity from the work of geographer Claire Dwyer who studies issues of identity in young British Muslim women. In one essay Dwyer explores the complexity around one group of young women's choices of dress or style. In that "Asian clothes" or traditional Muslim clothes, such as the Shalwar Kameez, are "highly significant markers of difference" (Dwyer, 1998, p. 54) in Western contexts, these choices can have important effects. Witness, for example, the ban on Muslim headscarves in French and British schools in 2004. The main issue is how these markers of identity are read in particular contexts. The girls Dwyer interviewed in the early 1990s were struggling with assumptions about Muslim culture and Muslim women circulating in British culture and media (for example, that Muslim women are repressed and subservient), while the headscarf issue is in part in response to post-9/11 representations of Muslims as terrorists and religious extremists. But these girls not only have to negotiate the dominant culture's assumptions of the meanings of their dress (especially at school or out in public), but also negotiate the expectations of their family and community. Therefore, how they appear on the street in their community has repercussions as well. Dwyer writes, "it is through a monitoring of the dress of young women, particularly in the streets of the neighborhood, that the cultural integrity of the community is upheld" (1998, p. 55). Therefore, not only does the dress have different meanings for different audiences, those meanings shift depending on the particular space or territory the young women are in.

> Although in many discussions participants would distinguish between "Western clothes" and "Asian clothes" they often sought to challenge the meanings associated with this dichotomy. Thus while many agreed that they might wear different clothes at school from those that they wore at home they denied that wearing different clothes in different places had any special significance. (Dwyer, 1998, p. 55)

For example, choice in clothes often depends on what's clean, what's ironed, what the weather is, what one's mood is, and so on. Some challenge Western assumptions by developing hybrid styles of dress. And some challenge the assumptions of the Muslim community by disarticulating the requirements of Muslim dress from particular styles and cultural traditions (for example, a long skirt covers as well as Shalwar Kameez). But some are also quite strategic in their use of dress. Some note that if they wear "Western clothes" in the neighborhood the community assumes that they're breaking any number of orthodox Muslim rules (whether or not they are), but if they dress traditionally in the neighborhood they can get away with breaking any number of rules (such as going out with boys). The question of dress is a question of territorialization and raises a number of complex dimensions of territorialization, but importantly highlights the point that while these processes can be strategic, they are not always so, or even self-conscious.

Global Youth

What then of global youth? What does that mean in this context? On the one hand this could refer to youth mobility. Global tourism has become an important activity for affluent youth. But also immigration and other means of movement within the global ethnoscape mean that many youth are growing up outside the country of origin of their parents or grandparents, like the girls studied by Dwyer above. Globalization means increased diversity especially in urban areas, and diversity in terms of national origin as well as just ethnicity and race.

On the other hand global youth can refer to the use of the products of global culture (that is, globally circulated media products, clothing, technologies, and so on) by youth in their own territorializations. Let me give you an example. The film, *La Haine* (The Hate) was produced in France in 1995. The film does not depict the romantic Paris of most films set there, but the blighted public housing projects of Paris's suburbs where many immigrants are forced to live. The film focuses on a day in the life of three friends: one African, one Arabic, and one Jewish, all part of the youthscape of their project. Their school was burned down in a riot, there are no jobs, and no spaces for youth to gather without the constant harassment of the police. An impromptu hot dog stand on the roof of one building is unceremoniously shut down by the cops. Disenfranchised, aggrieved, surveilled, repressed, and ignored by a racist society these youth struggle to claim their own spaces. To do so many rely on US media products. One recites lines from the 1970s film *Taxi Driver*, inhabiting the persona of Travis Bickle as a means of getting by. Others draw on the hip hop culture of likewise aggrieved populations of African Americans in the US. Some breakdance, some play rap music. One, played by a French DJ of Moroccan descent, in a provocative and prescient act of positionality, blast's KRS-One's song "Sound of Da Police" (about the parallels between slavery and police aggression) out his window onto the common plaza, mixing and scratching the song on his soundsystem with a song by French chanteuse Edith Piaf ("Non, Je Ne Regrette Rien," which means, "No, I regret nothing").

Global youth is about youth using global resources to deal with local conditions. However, these local conditions, particularly the deterioration of urban environments are produced in part by global economic forces. Global forces work over the spaces of youth. Cindi Katz discusses this situation in her 1998 essay, "Disintegrating Developments: Global Economic Restructuring and the Eroding of Ecologies of Youth." Katz describes youth as being increasingly caught between two dimensions of globalization. On the one hand globalization means deindustrialization and a disruption of local economies – the decline of manufacturing in some regions and the rise of the service sector. She writes that the "concern is the disintegration of possibilities for meaningful work and the broader social contracts that have been associated with it" (p. 131). There is no longer a clear path for youth to follow to obtain a meaningful job within the local cultural context. Not only is there no guarantee of employment, but there is a significant disinvestment in social support and education which would better equip them for the new economic landscape. Against this bleak economic context youth are caught by another dimension of globalization – the circulation of media products and with them the culture-ideology of consumption. As Katz puts it, "the reach of these products has led to a transnational burgeoning of desire and a breathtaking heterogeneity of means to satisfy it" (p. 131). The dilemma is this: the propagation of this culture-ideology of consumption (remember Liechty's example of creating teens in Nepal) leads to increased desire for a successful (read: materialist) lifestyle which is denied them by the deteriorating economy.

Katz provides two case studies. The first is a village she calls Howa in rural Sudan. An international development project changed Howa from a subsistence economy to a cash economy. Crops with local use such as sorghum and sesame were replaced by cash crops such as cotton. The fields and woodlands were cleared, irrigated, and chemical herbicides and pesticides were introduced. These developments degraded the ability of the environment to support as many livestock and made previously routine essential activities like gathering wood much more labor intensive (with fewer trees, people traveled further for wood, and limited supply made them desired commodities). The increased labor demands of the household and of cash crop farming meant that youth had less time for school. Katz argues strongly that "in Howa, children and adolescents were not learning what they were likely to need to know in their adulthoods" (p. 133). Though they were learning a lot about modern farming, the limited numbers of tenant plots meant that once they were grown there would be no new field for them and no other prospect of agricultural employment. Youth and young adults then leave the village to move to urban areas. But Sudan's poor national economy would not provide them jobs even there.

Katz parallels this example of "the systematic disruption of social reproduction" (p. 130) with a second case study, that of New York City, in which she describes similar erosions of traditional economies for the working class (in this case the sharp reduction of shipping, manufacturing, and other traditional working class industries in the city) and disinvestment in education and social services. Without the prospect of stable employment, "political-economic shifts (many associated with global processes) render the knowledge acquisition of many young people moot" (p. 134). Whereas in Howa the results of these global shifts led to a blighted natural environment, in New York it is the urban environment that is blighted for working class youth – playgrounds, parks, and other public facilities were no longer healthy options for youth as many are in severe disrepair. Katz (1998, pp. 135–6) writes:

> The restricted access to the public environment, and with it many opportunities for forging and negotiating peer culture and acquiring the various social skills associated with these negotiations, is generally worse for girls than boys. . . . The construction of subjectivity and identity formation are inflected and seriously compromised by these uneven socio-spatial relations in the contemporary urban environment.

Anoop Nayak offers an instructive example of the construction of subjectivity under such conditions, in particular the construction of racial identity. Nayak (2003) studied the cultural responses of different groups of white working-class youth in impoverished areas of Newcastle in North-East England. This is a region of strong working class traditions centered on coal mining and shipbuilding. However both of these industries have shut down, challenging the area economically through massive unemployment and culturally through the disruption of tradition and identity linked to these industries. The region faced renewal in the 1990s with the establishment of a number of microelectronic manufacturing facilities by transnational corporations like Siemens, Fujitsu, and Samsung. But given the fickle, mobile nature of postmodern capitalism many of these shut down again within a few years. The economic environment of the region is unsettled, to say the least. Against the backdrop of these conditions, Nayak describes three different responses by white youth to this unstable environment. The first he labels a localist response. These are The Real Geordies, who rework and take pride in a traditional white male working class identity disarticulated from particular traditions of employment and rearticulated around football and drinking. This is a subculture with some limited possibilities for mobility and employment. The second response he labels a survivalist one. These are The Charver Kids, an underclass of the extremely poor, "white trash," who survive via integration into a criminal underground economy. The third response is a globalist response of white kids, called Wiggers, Wannabes, and White Negroes who actively utilize global black culture (music, styles, sports – basketball rather than football/soccer) in constructing their identities and territories. Though these latter most explicitly exploit cultural globalization, all three are local responses to global shifts in investment and immigration.

Cindi Katz's point in all this is not just to lament the eroding ecology of global youth, but to propose that youth itself might be an appropriate site "for a new kind of politics in which everyday life is a theoretical site" (1998, p. 136). A focus on youth might be not only a new way of theorizing cultural globalization but a site for an active politics to create better environments not only for youth but for society as a whole. Katz provides a number of examples of this new politics like self-help initiatives for communities to reclaim their environments and their youth. In Howa, the village had, on its own, constructed a system of pipes and pumps for water, decreasing the time and labor demands of household subsistence. This freed up youth, especially girls, to attend school – a new school was built, also by community initiative. The pumps and the school were part of a broader effort by the village to "help insure local vitality in the face of imposed change" (p. 138). This effort included local farmers struggling for the right to grow sorghum on development project land. Other examples include neighborhoods in New York coming together on their own to rebuild playgrounds and schoolyards.

Nayak's argument is that youth might be an appropriate site for a new understanding and politics of identity not just in diverse urban communities with large immigrant populations but for seeing a diversity of racial identity and positioning in seemingly homogeneous populations. I'm considering Katz's and Nayak's work together not just because of their common concern with youth in declining economic environments but also as a way of getting back to Katz's earlier point: youth in economic crisis may draw on a variety of cultural resources to make sense of and cope with their everyday lives. On the one hand, this means being tempted by images of a life one will never have, but on the other hand these cultural products must be more than just objects of temptation and frustration.

Globalization provides youth with any number of images, ideas, styles, and narratives on which to draw. These mediascapes, as Appadurai has termed them:

> tend to be image-centered, narrative-based accounts of strips of reality, and what they offer to those who experience and transform them is a series of elements (such as characters, plots, and textual forms) out of which scripts can be formed of imagined lives, their own as well as those of others living in other places. (Appadurai, 1996, p. 35)

Recall, for example, the youth in the film *La Haine*, living in and through an imaginary New York of *Taxi Driver* and hip hop. And the Teds of the 1950s appropriated elements of gangster, gambler, and western films (e.g., their use of the bootlace tie) into their image and imagined reality. Let me return to Liechty's work for two more examples.

Liechty (1995) ends his essay on youth and modernity in Kathmandu with two examples of such imagined lives. The first is Ramesh, a 21-year old heroin addict from a middle-class background acutely aware of a cultural disjuncture between Nepal and the West, constantly comparing himself, his life, and his environment with an imagined New York City. Liechty (1995, p. 185) writes:

Indeed, Ramesh was a special connoisseur of films, books, magazine articles – anything he could find – having to do with America, and particularly New York City. He knew all the city's boroughs and landmarks but he was especially intrigued by "the Bronx," a place he brought up again and again in our conversations. From dozens of tough-guy films and gangster or mafia novels, Ramesh had constructed a detailed image of a New York City street culture full of drugs, thugs, and gangs.

Ramesh's dream was to someday move to New York and live the life of his imagination. As Liechty puts it later (p. 186):

> Ironically, it seemed sometimes as though Ramesh already lived in New York. "The Bronx" in particular seemed to be a kind of shadow universe where his mind roamed while his body navigated the streets of Kathmandu. "The Bronx" – with its street-smarts and anti-heroic codes of valor – was often the standard of reality against which he measured his own existence.

Though this is perhaps an extreme example, Liechty points out that "Ramesh's attitudes and opinions rarely differed in *content* from those of his middle-class peers, only in intensity" (p. 185). Fictional images and stories of New York have certainly not replaced his reality on the streets of Kathmandu, but given him a means of coping with it, of moving through that space, of territorializing.

Liechty's second example is of 22-year old Suman, middle-classed and educated, who worked for a tourist company. Suman, Liechty argues, is caught between a past that has been made irrelevant (that is, a traditional hill village where he had been born – with its sense of tradition) and a future which seemed to be something "that arrives pre-assembled from foreign places" (1995, p. 189). The position Suman is in is that of having to view his culture and past through the lens of this foreign future. This is almost literally the case in that at one point he had to lead a tourist group to his home village, forcing him to see it and his relatives "through the eyes of foreign tourists" (p. 189). This sense of floating in, as Suman put it, "this nowhere place," the result of what Cindi Katz called the disruption of social reproduction, leaves Suman and other youth vulnerable to both interpersonal and commercialized peer pressure. The space of youth culture in

Kathmandu is contested, and the youth do have some agency, though Liechty worries that "few have the resources, confidence and cultural authority to construct their own alternative, non-mediated visions of valued, modern and Nepali selves" (p. 193).

Providing youth these resources is part of the political project of youthscapes,[1] and the new kind of politics of youth that Katz argues for. An exemplary project in this regards is the Haja Center in Seoul, Korea. Founded in the late 1990s by cultural anthropologist Cho Han Haejoang, and funded by the city of Seoul and Yonsei University, the Haja Center was proposed as a creative intervention into the deteriorating quality of youth's lives. Like many East Asian nations, South Korea is strongly conformist and authoritarian, especially when it comes to education. Children and adolescents' days are highly structured, with most of the focus on studying and cramming. A common quip in Korea is, "sleep four hours and pass, sleep five hours and fail" (Beech, n.d.). Even youth haircuts are highly regulated, though long hair is no longer subject to police scrutiny as it once was. In sharp contrast with the contemporary education system, Professor Cho created a space for individual personal expression and learning. Officially named the Seoul Youth Factory for Alternative Culture, the Center is known as Haja, which means "let's do it!" in Korean. Haja is an open creative cultural space as well as a model alternative school where youth self-initiate their own learning ("Upgrade Oneself" is one of the slogans of the center). Haja provides a number of resources for students' projects, organized around a number of "factories" or high-tech facilities: film and video production, web production, music production, and a design studio. Youth are encouraged to be producers and not simply consumers (what has been termed, "prosumers"). They dance, paint, write music, produce videos, exploring a myriad of styles and identities. There are also opportunities for entrepreneurship and work through what's called their "youth venture incubator." The goal is to support youth in finding or creating a place for themselves as a cultural workforce and as modern cultural citizens (Cho, n.d.). What Haja does is to create a space for creativity and community both at the center and online through a number of websites and bulletin boards. These are spaces of work and play, away from the stresses, expectations, and relationships of everyday life.

In a country that had little identifiable youth culture prior to the 1980s, Haja presents an opportunity to create youth cultures, mingling traditional Korean cultural practices with global forms, such as hip hop dance moves, rap, punk and so on. Indeed, Haja's promotional videos highlight these hybrid aspects, drawing on a mix of Western and Korean popular music to make their point. For example, snippets from Pink Floyd's "Another Brick in the Wall (part 2)" (a song about abusive teachers, the kids chant, "we don't need no education") and Third Eye Blind's "Semi-Charmed Life" ("I want something else . . .") are used as well as Korean rock songs ("what is it you really want," Shin Hae Chul sings).

Significantly, Haja is positioned in promotional materials as not just responding to the Korean situation (a post-Korean War emphasis on state-led industrialization and development; a school system based on college preparation with relatively few places for college freshmen, guaranteeing "failure" for many;[2] an increasingly disruptive, disrespectful, and disorderly classroom culture; and an increasing number of voluntary drop-outs who refuse to be part of the system) but to a global crisis in education. They see the crisis of education in Korea as part of a general crisis in education in industrialized countries (including the US). Part of the Haja project is also building networks of teachers and students with other schools and groups across Asia and the rest of the world. Cho (n.d.) wants Haja to be a place youth from all over seek out to "upgrade their lives." Haja is consciously then both a local and a global response to the eroding ecology of the global youthscape.

But I don't want to misrepresent the Korean context. Haja is far from the only site for youth culture in Korea. The affluence created by the rapid industrialization of the country in the 1960s and 1970s led to the rise of a middle and upper-middle class, and that, plus a strong democratization movement in the 1980s, led to a consumer culture by the 1990s. The children of these families, raised in affluence with access to high end consumer goods and international travel, began creating spaces of their own in the early 1990s. This new youth subculture was referred to as the Orange Tribe; the most notorious place that they gathered was the district of Apgujungdong, especially in the cul-de-sac unofficially referred to by the English name, Rodeo Street. There, global retailers created a zone of consumption bathed in bright neon. Rodeo Street was the place for wealthy youth (and youth looking for a wealthy boyfriend or girlfriend) to hang out, shop, drink coffee or orange juice, see and be seen. Such conspicuous consumption flew in the face of the culture of thrift and austerity carefully cultivated during Korea's industrialization. The Orange Tribe were roundly critiqued in the press as being both immoral and victims of Westernization. That is, they were portrayed as being in that familiar category of youth-as-problem, deviants heavily into drugs, sex, and Western goods.

However, despite these portrayals, most encounters were much more chaste than was implied in the news reports. For sociologist Rob Shields (1997), what was scandalous for Korean culture about Apgujungdong and the Orange Tribe was the directness of the social contact between strangers, especially men and women. Evenings were filled with conversation and sociability. A new generation of cultural studies scholars in Korea, including Cho Han Haejoang who later founded the Haja Center, saw Apgujungdong and similar areas "as a new kind of 'polysemic' cultural site and 'event space' in which youth and young urban professionals performed 'strong self-expressions' through styles and non-traditional social behavior" (Lee, 2006, p. 101). There youth transgressed "social grammars" in their desire "to escape from the constraint of Korean daily life" (p. 101). In other words, "youth successfully created their own cultural territories, thereby empowering themselves" (p. 117). These gatherings were a creative force, a specific territorialization drawing on and responding to a particular cultural, social, economic moment in Korea. The Haja Center can be seen as one attempt to articulate that creative force to a specific set of social issues around education, individual self-empowerment, and democracy. As we'll see in the next chapter, other spaces in Seoul opened up at this time that embodied other youth responses. These other spaces, around Hongik University for example, were not home to a single subculture but provided multiple cultural responses within the same space (punk, hip hop, and so on). These spaces are liminal spaces, meaning that they are at the limit of a culture, at the edge where a culture abuts other cultures.

The liminal space of Rodeo Street, Rob Shields argues, is not some global or Western space, set apart from Korean culture. It is not a carbon copy of similar looking high streets in the West, but is very much embedded in and responsive to Korean culture from the arrangement of stores and services to the teeming dance of social relationships (and flirting) in the crowds on the street, the particular intermingling of groups of men and women.

Core and Periphery

The affluent youth of Apgujungdong seem not to need the resources provided by Haja or argued for by Cindi Katz. Theirs seems an expanding world of travel and consumption and they don't seem victims of the peripheral consciousness Liechty so vividly describes in Nepal. But we need to mention that peripheral is always a relative term. Periphery usually implies a "core," and core–periphery models are common in theories of globalization. Such models are usually described from the perspective of the core (argue Hilary Pilkington and Ul'iana Bliudina (2002)) and rarely from the perspective of the periphery. Sociologist Hilary Pilkington argues for a reorientation of both globalization studies and youth culture studies to examine closely the experience of youth at the so-called periphery (Pilkington and Johnson, 2003; Pilkington et al., 2002). Peripheralist perspectives "require the reinstatement of the peripheral subject as an active agent in globalization" (Pilkington and Bliudina, 2002, p. 3). But to do so is to recognize that the position of a peripheral subject is always multidimensional and complex.

For example, Dannie Kjeldgaard (2003) studied high school youth in Denmark and Greenland, comparing youth in both rural and urban contexts in each place. Greenland is a part of Denmark, though it has home rule. In many ways it is a periphery to the core of Denmark. Kjeldgaard found that though in urban Copenhagen youth's "discourses of identity and consumption were found to be organized around the construction and articulation of a narrative of self, particularly concerning authenticity" (p. 290) in which they discussed how to construct identity from the choices available, youth in the more rural Danish city of Svendborg focused on their lack of choice and the paucity of opportunities to consume. That is, urban youth focused on style and identity while rural youth (on the periphery) focused more on the nature of locality and the variability of the consumptionscape (that

71

is, there were less opportunities to consume where they were). However, in Greenland youth focused more on discourses of collective identity – that is, not who am I as an individual but who are we as Greenlanders (as opposed to Danish)? Discourses of identity had to do with creating and maintaining a local cultural identity (for example, closeness to nature). Global cultural products were bought not to create or maintain a social position but opportunistically. Kjeldgaard describes the consumptionscape of global products in Greenland as ephemeral; things become available for short periods of time. At the same time, access to television means that they desire these products even more. So while on the one hand youth in Greenland exhibit a strong local ethnic and cultural identity (for example, versus Denmark which is not seen as having access to nature in the same way as Greenland), on the other hand their identity in terms of consumption is predicated on a discourse of lack. "There's really nothing here," one student says (p. 299). However, while youth in urban Greenland see lack of opportunities to consume, youth in rural Greenland see even less (and look with envy on those who live in the capital city, Nuuk). Peripheries are always centers to other peripheries. But not all youth in Greenland see themselves within this discourse of deprivation. One informant sees her life as similar to youth in other locations (with whom she corresponds over the Internet): "we sleep, we watch television, we listen to music, we party and go to school" (p. 300). Through such a pragmatic perspective, life in Greenland seems "normal," a significant "*ideological break* with the notion of difference and deprivation (lack)" (p. 300, emphasis in original).

Let me give you one more example about the complexities of the positioning of peripheral youth, this time from Russia. Pilkington and Bliudina remind us that practices of consumption and reception of global media and products don't just happen but happen within specific economic, social, and historical structures. This means, for example, that it's not just location (as Kjeldgaard discussed above) but social class that is an important factor (remember the affluent youth of Apgujungdong) in the availability of products and what meanings they take on. In addition, "[c]ultural messages from the West today are neither simply absorbed nor complexly reworked in isolation. Rather, such messages are filtered through state-level ideology and the experiences, memories, imaginations, and fantasies that accumulate individually and collectively" (Pilkington and Bliudina, 2002, p. 3). That is, Western products have to be seen in the light of Soviet and Russian history as both antagonists and alternatives to the West in terms of cultural values. Russia sees itself as unique and not necessarily part of Europe or the West. Globalization discourse is seen in many ways as a discourse of American imperialism; Russian scholars prefer to focus on Russia's place in the world rather than Russia's place within globalization. "Russia does not position itself as a 'peripheral receiver' of Western cultural messages but rather as the embodiment of alternative cultural values" (Pilkington and Bliudina, 2002, p. 13).

Within Russian youth cultures this means multiple responses (and multiple levels of response) to Western products. On the one hand youth envy the standards of living and quality of products from the West, but on the other hand they question the morality of that way of life.

> In the case of Russian youth, it is argued, globalization is welcomed insofar as it accelerates the eradication of Russia's isolated past and presents opportunities to realize levels of material comfort existing at globalization's "core." While young Russians aspire to Western standards of living, however, they do not seek to emulate Western standards of "being"; and where spiritual life is concerned, young people remain firmly rooted to the local. (Pilkington and Bliudina, 2002, p. 20)

Pilkington, writing with Elena Omel'chenko, argues that Russian youth don't see themselves as being left out of global culture, just that global culture seems a one way street, and they are only on the receiving end. In addition, they feel that global culture ignores, caricatures, or misunderstands Russia. So while the quality of Western goods is desired, there is also a desire for Russian goods to "catch up" in terms of quality. Western goods are a resource for Russian youth, but only one of many on which they draw. There is in addition a strong cultural heritage and sense of "soulfulness" which is seen as lacking in the West (and in Western products). The "Russian cultural space that young people inhabited might be better visualized as a giant 'mix and match' counter in which the global and the local existed simultaneously" (Pilkington and Omel'chenko, 2002, p. 211). Russians are seen as taking Western cultural products (for example, rock music) and making something Russian from them. Russian rock is not seen as a hybrid cultural form, but as something Russian (expressing the Russian soul). Russia's uniqueness triumphs. So though there are some who see Russia's public cultural space becoming globalized, Westernized, and indeed Americanized, Pilkington concludes that youth do not seem as concerned. They see the difference between Western products (which are fun and have their uses) and Russian ones. She writes, "young people were happy to *consume* Western ('other,' 'global') culture, while remaining confident that that which was Russian ('ours,' 'local') would remain untarnished by global intrusion" (2002, p. 225). Indeed, youth argue that Russian culture has not globalized simply because it has its particular value which "could not be understood outside Russia" (p. 225). So though Russian culture could be seen to be peripheral to the global Western core, Russian youth seem to exhibit a very different form of peripheral consciousness, one which challenges the valorization of the core, the West, and the global. Indeed, global culture is made relative, which is as it should be.

Global youth are those that territorialize with non-local connections. These connections are products and other objects (and sounds, scents, and tastes) that open one up to spaces elsewhere. Connections, as Massey pointed out, are social, fraught with power – which is unequal – and contingent. These spaces/territories/homes of global youth are always local rearticulations of cultures, meanings, habits, and products. The case studies here represent different balances and configurations of habitus and flows of foreign culture. Globalization is the awareness of these distant connections, an awareness of the simultaneity of the world. That awareness becomes a form of peripheral consciousness depending on the particular relation between the other place(s) and one's own home. One is more victimized by peripheral consciousness if one doesn't have the means to do anything about it. Wealthy youth in industrialized Korea can consume and shop. Youth in nonindustrialized Nepal and Greenland have varying responses. In Greenland, a strong local culture and ethnic identity helps relativize the peripheral consciousness. Whereas in Nepal, Liechty seems to indicate that urban youth have been cut off from family and tradition, more adrift and despairing perhaps than their peers elsewhere.

In either case, youth are still territorializing, making do in varying economic, social, and cultural conditions. In some places, like Korea, youth are challenging the established culture and are afforded the resources (cultural or economic) to do so and envision a future. In other situations, like those Katz, Liechty, or Nayak describe, globalization has severely disrupted the economic stability of the area, eliminating hopes of succeeding as one's parents did, eliminating the resources one needs to provide a local future. In all cases, globalization has provided a set of cultural resources used in various ways, seen as culturally destructive by the parent culture (the critiques of teens in Kathmandu echo the critiques of the Orange Tribe in Seoul), which youth draw on to a greater or lesser extent simply to get by. These cultural resources can be wildly at odds with the realities of local conditions – recall Dorfman and Mattelart's warning from the previous chapter that the values of individualism and personal consumption are antiproductive in an economically strapped context like that of a Third World nation.

Globalization ultimately relativizes the world, establishing a complex network of relationships between sites, some seen as centers, some as peripheries; some peripheries seen as centers to other peripheries, and so on. It is this complex network of relationships which youth (and indeed all of us) have to learn to negotiate in an ethical way and which a focus on global youthscape helps to illuminate.

Notes

1   *Youthscapes* is a term I borrow from Sunaina Marr Maira and Elisabeth Soep (2005) who propose the term as a means of bringing together questions of globalization, politics, power, and culture focused around youth and their experiences. That is, they propose that the examination of the terrain of youth globally is an important means to understand the multifarious issues of globalization.

2   Cultural Studies scholar Keehyeung Lee (2006, p. 112) writes: "Considering the fact that out of almost half a million college applicants only less than twenty thousand students are admitted into these top universities, the anxiety level of youth in high school runs high."

4

Global Music

I've been listening to what we could call global music in some form
or other most of my life. Though I grew up in Southeast Asia, South
Asia, and the Middle East, the music that surrounded me – that played
in our house – was predominantly American. My parents had their
LP records (Frank Sinatra, Andy Williams, Perry Como) and mix tapes
of current hits recorded on reel-to-reel tapes by friends and relatives
back in the States (later supplemented by cassettes purchased in
Hong Kong and Taiwan, which were probably pirated). We encountered non-US music locally as folk music rather than as popular music.
Otherwise, our dabblings with non-US music was filtered through
the trends of mainstream Western popular music: Latin flavors in jazz
(Herb Alpert, Cal Tjader, The Baja Marimba Band) or the odd
break-out hit (we had Miriam Makeba's first LP). It was only when
my sister and I were older that we started listening to more locally
generated pop. In the early 1970s, when living in India, I don't recall
listening to the radio at all, just our own isolated audiobubble of LPs
and reel-to-reels. Then, in Korea, we listened only to Armed Forces
Radio with its stream of US pop hits ("Billy Don't be a Hero" and
so on). And later, in the Philippines in the late 1970s, where US-flavored
pop and Eurodisco seem to have infused and shaped the local pop
scene, we started listening to local radio. So we became fans of
Freddie Aguilar, Basil Valdez, Rico J. Puno.

It wasn't until I was in my twenties, living in the US, that I began
exploring more "world music" (generally, non-Western music consumed in the West – we'll get into definitions in a moment), though

this was also mediated through Western popular music and musicians. In high school a number of friends were into art rock, especially Rush and Genesis. I began listening to Peter Gabriel (former lead singer for Genesis) especially as he began collaborating and touring with African musicians like Youssou N'Dour and later Papa Wemba. I found his phenomenally popular album *So* influential, as was Paul Simon's controversial *Graceland* LP – both of which got me exploring African popular music on my own (though guided by Gabriel's Real World record label which released selected non-Western albums).

I didn't like all African music, just some. For example, though I have tremendous respect for Fela Kuti, I don't play his CDs. And I don't like African music just because it's African or just because Peter Gabriel's company released it. But this began a careful consideration of why I was listening to what I was. This chapter raises a number of questions about listening habits, the circulation of global music, the exploitation of non-Western musicians, the mediation of non-Western music by Western artists and record companies, and the perils and racisms of bourgeois aural tourism. All of which made me reflect carefully on my own choices. For myself, I realized that I liked what I liked because I liked the space. I liked the space they created or how it altered me as I moved through it, be it Beethoven, Rush, or Papa Wemba. However, I've done enough reading (and hung out with enough critical music scholars) to know that aesthetics isn't everything, to be wary of the exploitative machinations of the global music industry, to become aware of the local and global political struggles that particular songs and musics are responding to. But for me, space comes first: I can't like a song by its politics alone, though I can dislike a song because of its politics, and I can also ignore some politics if I really like a song (for example Rush base a number of songs on the writings of Ayn Rand, whom I dislike politically, but I like the songs). This aural territorialization is cultural, economic, and political; it is both socially structured and intensely personal. Music scholar Josh Kun calls the territorialization by music *audiotopia*: "music is experienced not only as sound that goes into our ears and vibrates through our bones but as a space that we enter into, encounter, move around in, inhabit, be safe in, learn from" (Kun, 2005, p. 2). The issues of that space are what we are exploring in this chapter.

Therefore, this chapter addresses the question of music in a global context for a number of reasons. First, the last chapter focused on globalization and a particular population (youth). It makes sense, then, to complement that effort with a focus on a particular cultural form, music. Second, music is one important way that people territorialize – they shape the space they're in with rhythms, sounds, meanings. This not only is a communicative act (expresses their identity to those around, and to oneself) but also an affective one, since we use music as well to alter our own bodily states, our mood, our affect, our intensity. And we use music to claim a space (regardless, at times, of what meanings it has – it's good music if it makes people leave you alone, or attracts only certain types of people into a group, and so on). Third, the global music industry is a fairly clear case, from a political economy perspective, of cultural imperialism – dominated as it is by European and Japanese corporations and American artists and music forms. As Pilkington and Bliudina (2002, p, 14) put it: "The American popular music industry, for example, has experienced such extensive transnationalization that it has undermined domestic industries in almost all other countries and acted as a medium for the transmission of a wider set of American youth and African-American cultural styles." At the same time, music is a complex realm that provides numerous examples of the reworking of global musical forms to respond to, resonate with, local meanings, conditions, and events. James Lull (1995) referred to this process as that of cultural reterritorialization.

By *global music* I simply mean music that circulates globally. It's a too-simple term for a quite dynamic and uneven terrain. Like many mass media, discourse about global music has been dominated by discussions of cultural imperialism which tend to oversimplify the situation. How I'd like to proceed in this chapter is to address the debates about the cultural imperialism of (and through) music and the exploitative relationship between Western and non-Western musics. Then I want to open up these debates using the more complex model of globalization developed in Chapter 2, in particular addressing Appadurai's notion of scapes and Wilk's notion of structures of common difference. We'll end by spending some time on the global circulation of punk and hip hop as influential cultural forms.

World Music and Cultural Imperialism

World Music is a category of music in the West that tends to encompass non-Western musical artists, especially so-called traditional musics (see Barrett, 1996; Feld, 1994, 2000; Goodwin and Gore, 1995; Roberts, 1992; Sakolsky, 1995, Stone, 2006). It is a category found in music magazines and record stores. It is generally a North American phenomenon, and is clearly a genre constructed from a North American perspective. Traditional music of North America is categorized as folk (unless it is the music of indigenous populations or certain ethnic groups, like Zydeco). The World Music genre includes anthropological recordings (Songs of the Pygmies), traditional music (Brazilian folk songs, classical Indian sitar music), non-US popular music (Edith Piaf, Zap Mama, Clannad – though other Irish groups like U2 and the Cranberries are over in Pop/Rock), non-US dance-oriented music (Afropop collections, Bhangra, Japanese pop collections, Buena Vista Social Club CDs), touristic collections of pop music (Rough Guides to any number of particular genres), and hybrid music, which integrates a variety of non-Western and Western musics and musicians (Afro-Celt Soundsystem). However, dabblings with non-Western musics and musicians, if done by a major US or European artist (like Peter Gabriel, Paul Simon, or Sting) does not get categorized here. World music, therefore, caters to middle-class aural tourism, problematic (at times racist) desire for authentic, tribal, or primitive music (which frames these musicians and peoples as primitive, primal, as well), and (to a much less extent) immigrant or expatriate communities.

> The pop-music industry's packaging of exotic cultures for western consumption, it might be claimed, is just the musical equivalent of what has been going on for decades in the tourist industry, that is, listening to world music is a form of musical tourism whose function, like that of tourism, is to give consumers the illusion of authentic engagement with other cultures while in fact insulating them from their more sober political and economic realities. (Roberts, 1992, p. 233)

World music also gets labeled as International Music (though only certain international acts are included – the British Rolling Stones aren't here, for example, and neither is Dave Matthews, who is from South Africa), World Beat (a focus on dance music), Ethnopop, and so on.

Music scholar Andrew Goodwin and Joe Gore, editor of *Guitar* magazine, explore some of the relevant debates around "world beat" and cultural imperialism. Critical scholarship on world beat tends to fall into one of two camps, they argue: world beat is exploitation of Third World musicians or world beat is resistant and subversive, the Third World talking back and infiltrating the Western music establishment. The situation is, of course, more complicated than this. There are clear cases of the exploitation of Third World musicians by Western musicians. Non-Western musicians provide cheap labor – ill-paid for their efforts and creativity – while Western performers retain the credit, royalties, and copyright. Malcolm McLaren, for example, claims "composer credits for two sections of traditional (indeed *sacred*) Afro-Cuban music, 'Obatala' and 'Legba'" on his album *Duck Rock* (Goodwin and Gore, 1995, p. 126). Perhaps the most debated example is Paul Simon's 1986 album *Graceland*, which he recorded substantially in South Africa with local musicians, including the group Ladysmith Black Mambazo. George Lipsitz (1994) summarizes the controversy by making the following points: On the one hand, Simon's album provided exposure for these artists to the West (launching the international career of Ladysmith), demonstrated racial cooperation during the era of Apartheid, paid the musicians above scale, and shared composer credits and royalties. On the other hand, Simon defied an anti-Apartheid boycott of South Africa to record the album, providing the South African government with a public relations bonanza, retained copyright (it is a Paul Simon album, in the end, and not a collective),[1] and in arranging his songs he stripped music and lyrics of their local connotations (about black struggle under a racist government, for example) and used them as exotic accompaniment for his own "lyrics about cosmopolitan postmodern angst" (Lipsitz, 1994, p. 57). Lipsitz argues that it's not that Simon (and others such as David Byrne) shouldn't reach out creatively to world musicians but that he needs "a self-conscious understanding of unequal power relations, of the privileges available to Anglo-American recording stars because of the economic power of the countries from which they come" (p. 61). In the end, Lipsitz writes, Simon "remains so preoccupied with what cross-cultural contact means for him, that he neglects addressing what it might mean to others" (p. 60).[2]

British musician Peter Gabriel tends to be more cognizant of the issues of appropriation when he composes music (Taylor, 1997, p. 50), seeking balance, cooperation, and dialogue. He often showcases non-Western sources of his own music on accompanying albums. For example his soundtrack for the film, *The Last Temptation of Christ*, *Passion*, was accompanied by *Passion Sources*; his album *Us* by *Plus from Us*. And he is a strong promoter of non-Western musicians through his own record label, Real World, and organizations such as WOMAD (World of Music, Arts, and Dance). However, like Simon, he sees only the aesthetic dimensions of the music (it's all about the tunes and the creativity) and what he can make of it, which strips the music (and the situation of the creation of his own work) of its politics and makes the unfamiliar palatable to Western ears. Music scholar Timothy Taylor gives the example of the opening track to Gabriel's *Passion* album, "The Feeling Begins." This track begins with an Armenian doudouk playing in traditional style, free and without meter. But soon the song imposes a regular 4/4 meter on the doudouk. "This repackaging of time marks one of the most salient impositions of western concepts on the musics of other cultures" (Taylor, 1997, p. 41).

If non-Western music makes it to the ears of Western listeners, it is often attributed solely to the agency (and generosity) of Western musicians and record producers. Steve Feld (2000) calls this the "popstar curation" of world music. Indeed it seems that it is the Westerner's burden to rescue or save these musics from extinction (since they wouldn't be saved by themselves, presumably). A case in point is American guitarist Ry Cooder's "rescue" of a group of pre-revolutionary Cuban musicians and their establishment back in their rightful place on the world stage in the album and documentary, *The Buena Vista Social Club*. However, as Tanya Katerí Hernández (2002) argues, such colonialist narratives of discovery and rescue ignore the role of Cuban musician Juan de Marcos González who had been gathering the musicians together for a separate project prior to Cooder's arrival in Cuba (on another project which fell through). They also misrepresent the situations of the musicians themselves and their music, son. For example, singer Ibrahim Ferrer is depicted as having to shine shoes to make a living, abandoned as he was by the Cuban music establishment and audiences. Actually Ferrer was living on a government pension and was only shining shoes because he was restless and bored in his retirement. Son music was portrayed as being likewise abandoned and forsaken despite the fact that it is regularly performed and even supported by the Cuban government as part of Cuba's national heritage (see also Brennan, 2003).

One side effect of Western musician's promotion of particular music and musicians is the impact this has on local music. Paul Simon's promotion of Ladysmith Black Mambazo increased demand for that style of township music to the detriment of other more modern styles. Ry Cooder's promotion of the Buena Vista Social Club elevated son and ignores and eclipses modern Cuban music and its political dimensions.

A notorious case of the appropriation of a non-Western song is the history of Solomon Linda's song, popularly referred to as "Wimoweh" (LaFraniere, 2006; Milan, 2000; Verster, 2005). In 1939, South African singer Linda and his group recorded a song called, "Mbube," which means "The Lion" in Zulu. The song became a hit, selling 100,000 copies (unprecedented for an African record at that time), and gained international notice. American folk singer Pete Seeger recorded a version in the 1950s (mistakenly hearing the word "mbube" as "wimoweh"), which became a standard. In the 1960s the group The Tokens recorded a version which focused on a short improvisation at the end of the original version, making that its main musical theme, and which introduced new words. The new version was called "The Lion Sleeps Tonight." Linda had sold the rights to the song in the 1930s for less than $1. Over the years he and his family had seen a few royalties from the various recordings of the song (over 150 cover versions have been recorded by artists from REM to Nanci Griffith, reaping an estimated $15 million in profits over the years (Milan, 2000)), but never enough to pull them out of bitter poverty, even after the song was included in the internationally successful Disney film, *The Lion King*. It was only after a 2000 *Rolling Stone* article about the injustice that more adequate compensation began to be provided to Linda's family (Linda having died in 1962). The history of "Mbube" and "The Lion Sleeps Tonight" is fraught with legal battles, not only between Linda's family and US music publishers, but between the various music publishers themselves. In the end, as Rian Milan argues in his groundbreaking article in *Rolling Stone*, the case of "Mbube" is not a legal one (Linda *did* sell his rights to the song to the record company) but a moral one that echoes the long exploitation of black artists by white artists and recording companies.

To return to Goodwin and Gore's argument, one problem with the idea of cultural imperialism is that it assumes that the empire and the colony are different to begin with, that the empire imposes something foreign (music, film, etc.) on a local context, or that a local text (song, tune, rhythm) appropriated for use in the empire is something completely foreign and unknown to that empire. But this is not often the case in music. For example, Paul Simon has said that he was attracted to the sound of South African music because "it sounded like very early rock and roll to me, black, urban, mid-fifties rock and roll" (quoted in Feld, 1994, p. 241). Steve Feld (1994, p. 241) notes:

> Of course, the reason it sounded that way had much to do with the steady stream of African-American rhythm and blues records that have circulated in South Africa and the way South African pop styles emerged in the context of a record industry with strong links to the American jazz, blues, gospel, and soul markets.

Such international borrowings must also be put within the broader context of a long history of white performers mediating black music. For example, Elvis popularized R&B, the Rolling Stones popularized the blues, and Eric Clapton popularized the blues (covering Richard Johnson's germinal song, "Crossroads") and reggae (through his cover of Bob Marley's "I Shot the Sherriff"). George Lipsitz writes, "White Americans have demonstrated many times a pathological need to control, contain, and even take credit for Black culture" (1994, p. 54).

In another example, The Talking Heads were inspired by the music of Fela Kuti, Nigerian Afro-Beat, for their album, *Remain in Light*. However, Kuti had attended Trinity College of Music in London and had spent a year in Los Angeles (becoming friends with Black Panther activist Sandra Isidore) (Lipsitz, 1994; Stapleton and May, 1990). He was also famously influenced by James Brown (Feld, 1994; Goodwin and Gore, 1995). James Brown himself had been reworking African polyrhythms in his own music (Feld, 1994).

So when Western musicians and audiences turn to African popular music to find "roots," they find a diverse set of musics with hundreds of years of cross-Atlantic influence. The introduction of Western musical instruments to Africa preceded even colonialism (Stapleton and May, 1990). But with colonialism came military brass bands playing polkas and marches. In the early nineteenth century troops and musicians from the Caribbean were stationed in West Africa, bringing with them Caribbean music. Christian missionaries introduced European styles of harmony, melody, rhythm, and instrumentation as well as hymns, classical music, and Negro spirituals. Both the Caribbean music and spirituals were, of course, initially created by African slaves integrating African musical sensibilities with an imposed Christianity. By the late nineteenth century urban elites in Africa were sponsoring classical choirs and symphonies. Guitars were introduced by sailors and influential guitar styles spread from port cities inland. Radio was established in the 1920s and records had been widely circulating by this time. A worldwide boom in Latin music, especially of Cuban rumbas, boleros, and mambos, took hold in Africa in the 1930s perhaps because this was a music that itself had African roots (Stapleton and May, 1990). The first recording studio in sub-Saharan Africa was established in Johannesburg by an Italian playboy hoping to sell American hillbilly music and local covers (in local languages) of hillbilly tunes (Milan, 2000). That is where Solomon Linda recorded "Mbube." And so on. I should emphasize here that Africa is a diverse continent and the histories of musics are likewise locally specific.

> Paul Gilroy argues in his book *The Black Atlantic* (Gilroy, 1993) that, if you wanted to tell the story of black music, you wouldn't construct a story of how "authentic" black music *started* in Africa and became diluted with each subsequent transformation – the blues, reggae, Afro-Cuban, jazz, soul and rap – all representing "loss of tradition" the further the music gets dispersed from its *roots*. Instead, you would have to pay attention to the way black music has traveled across and around the diaspora by many, overlapping *routes*. (Hall, 1995, p. 207)

Despite the hybrid nature of most of the world's musics, there is pressure placed on non-Western artists to remain "authentic," not to "sell out." Indeed, the label "world music" at times presumes or guarantees a certain authenticity (Feld, 2000). The demand to be authentic is an *essentialist* view of identity (see Chapter 1), which argues that individuals and groups have "natural" affinities to particular musics or rhythms. Senegalese singer Youssou N'Dour, who has recorded with both Simon and Gabriel, has been accused by critics of catering to Western audiences and altering his sound to match Western tastes. Ironically, N'Dour is also known for his efforts in reviving local traditional music in Senegal. When Gabriel or Simon explore foreign music, they are called artists. N'Dour, likewise, is an artist, but the resistance to his musical explorations by the Western music press reveals a double standard for non-Western artists. Timothy Taylor (1997, p. 126) asserts that musicians like N'Dour "are moderns who face constant pressure from westerners to remain musically and other-wise premodern – that is, culturally 'natural' – because of racism and western demands for authenticity."

An interesting example of answering back to Western appropriations of non-Western music is that of Cameroonian musician Manu Dibango's 1994 album, *Wakafrika*. Dibango, a renowned jazz saxophonist, keyboard player, and arranger, is known in the US for his 1972 hit, "Soul Makossa." For *Wakafrika* Dibango assembled an all-star list of African musical talent: Youssou N'Dour, Ladysmith Black Mambazo, Geoffrey Oryema, Salif Keita, Ray Lema, Ray Phiri, King Sunny Adé, Angélique Kidjo, Papa Wemba, and others. The album is an interesting selection of primarily covers. The album not only covers internationally known African hits like Dibango's own "Soul Makossa," Fela Kuti's "Lady," and Miriam Makeba's "Pata Pata," but mainstays of Western collaboration and appropriation such as Peter Gabriel's "Biko," Paul Simon's "Homeless," and Solomon Linda's "Wimoweh." "Biko" is a song about the death of anti-apartheid activist Stephen Biko at the hands of South African police in 1977. Gabriel would perform the song in concert in the 1980s as a rousing call to end apartheid and for the release of fellow activist Nelson Mandela from prison. Dibango's version was recorded three years after Mandela's release and the collapse of apartheid. This post-apartheid version features a more upbeat rhythm than Gabriel's more solemn chant. Dibango's version retains Gabriel's voice, but as part of the background mix, where non-Western singers are often relegated on Western records. "Homeless" is perhaps the most balanced of the collaborations on Simon's *Graceland* album. Simon shares songwriting credit with Ladysmith's Joseph Shambala and details the collaboration, and each of their contributions, in *Graceland's* liner notes. Significantly, it is the one song on the album that does not feature Simon singing his "lyrics about cosmopolitan postmodern angst" (Lipsitz, 1994, p. 57). Finally, Dibango performs Solomon Linda's song as "Wimoweh" rather than the original "Mbube." This is either an ignorant slip or a commentary on cross-cultural appropriation. In support of the latter interpretation, he credits "Wimoweh" to Linda and Paul Campbell. Campbell does not exist; the name was an alias used by the Weavers' managers when they re-arranged and copyrighted folk and traditional songs (like "Hush Little Baby") which weren't owned by anyone (Milan, 2000). The Weaver's version of "Wimoweh" was released bearing just Campbell's name as composer. By listing both names, Dibango incorporates the Weavers' appropriation and its African original.

Global Flows of Music

In this discussion of cultural imperialism and music, we've been focusing for coherency's sake primarily on Western appropriations of African music. Western musicians also appropriate the music of other regions as well (for example, Simon's borrowing of Peruvian flute music in Simon and Garfunkel's "El Condor Pasa"). Each borrowing deserves more discussion than we have space for here, but we should be cognizant of particular trends within Western popular music (Latin flavors in pop music like Shakira, the Indian rhythms of bhangra, the sudden presence of North African rai singers – such as Cheb Mami collaborating with Sting on "Desert Rose" – and so on). We should be aware of what these sounds are made to mean within pop music as they are reduced to particular exotic essences (for example, what is the sound of a Celtic harp supposed to mean to the audience? Or African drums? Or Indian sitar? Or Latin rhythms? Heat? Exoticism? Fantasy? Mystery?). And we should ask how these relations between sounds relate to cultural and economic relations between regions (why bhangra or rai *now*?).

The discussion of appropriation is only a sliver of the cultural imperialism debate. We could spend the rest of this book on the global circulation of Western music, ownership of the music industry, the popularity of Western acts abroad, and so on; in short, how Western music has colonized the world's soundscape – the flows, interchanges, and cross-cultural influences that have been occurring for centuries. And then there's music videos, the global presence of MTV . . . we could go on. Though on the one hand, and at first blush, the global music scene seems incorporated and prepackaged by transnational corporations, the global airwaves and record shelves overflowing with Western artists, we need to remember a couple of things. First, we can't proceed on the logic of displacement, as Wilk has argued (1995). That is, we can't argue that the importation of Western goods (songs, CDs, and so on) *necessarily* displaces local music. Audiences are capable of listening to both. The presence of Western music on local playlists doesn't in itself prove imperialism (Tomlinson, 1991, 1999). What does Western music mean to those listening? Are these songs the most popular? Why or why not? (See our discussions of the flows of J-dramas in Chapter 2.) Second, given all the cross-cultural borrowing (for example between North America and Africa over the past number of centuries), what is considered "Western" music is debatable, at least.

To get a broader sense of the flows involved in global music than that offered by cultural imperialist views, let's look at global music in terms of Appadurai's scapes (discussed in Chapter 2). I'm also following Martin Roberts' (1992) framing of these key issues. One of the most prominent scapes to consider in this regard is ethnoscape, the movement of people. As people move, their music moves with them. The movement of diasporic peoples changes not only their music but the music of the places they move to and through. The musical impact of African slaves on the musics of the Americas is perhaps the most obvious example, but there are other migrations as well: Latino populations to the US; Indians to Asia, Africa, the Middle East, and the US; Chinese throughout Asia, Europe, and North America, and so on. These immigrant populations represent potential audiences for these musics. We could also consider the movement of colonial troops and merchants. But world musicians move as well, for education (Fela Kuti studied in England), work (N'Dour lives in London, Dibango lives in Paris), touring, or other reasons (including exile – Ugandan Geoffrey Oryema lives in political exile in Paris; Gilberto Gil lived in exile for a time in London).

Technoscape, the landscape of technology, is also prominent here. On the one hand, as Roberts (1992) points out, high quality production facilities in New York, London, Paris, and Los Angeles make them important meeting places for global musicians. However, the cost of such production equipment has decreased dramatically allowing for more regional record production – though regional production has existed for quite a while (Solomon Linda recorded "Mbube" in Johannesburg, after all, though the recording had to be shipped to London to be mastered and pressed into records). Technoscape also includes the movement of musical instruments (like the brass instruments introduced to Africa by colonial powers; the guitar introduced there by sailors), broadcast technologies (e.g., radio), and playback machines (tape players, MP3 players, and so on).

Finanscape points to the concentration of the music industry by a handful of conglomerates, the "Big Four": EMI (UK), Warner Music (US), Sony/Bertelsmann Music Group (BMG) (Japan and Germany), and Vivendi Universal (France). The profits from a myriad of labels across the globe funnel, eventually, back to American, European, and Japanese financial centers. However, what this fact illuminates is that ownership does not determine music content, otherwise there would be a lot more Japanese, German, and French acts on the global music scene.

Mediascape points to the circulation and distribution of music media (tapes, CDs, MP3 files), networks of transmission (satellite TV channels for music videos), and the flow of content itself. These "complex audioscapes" as Roberts terms them, become the subject of the remainder of this chapter. "The overall effect of such transnational musical landscapes and the kind of musical literacy they produce has been increasingly to diversify musical cultures and problematize core/periphery, center/margin oppositions" (Roberts, 1992, p. 237).

For music scholar George Lipsitz, popular music is a way for people to use global networks of communication to speak to and of local conditions under globalization. Poor, disenfranchised, and postcolonial populations have experienced first-hand the consequences of globalization – the erosion of social support structures; the mobility of global capital investment (think of the waves of employment and unemployment in Newcastle caused by the establishment and abandonment of manufacturing plants discussed in the previous chapter); the tantalizing images of prosperity that flood the media, prosperity denied by local economic conditions; and the mobility of populations, driven by work, war, politics, and racism. People who can speak to and of these conditions become extremely valuable, Lipsitz argues, in helping us to understand and negotiate globalization. The cultural products produced by these populations, under these conditions, would not only provide a description and critique of globalization from within, but would also make others aware of local conditions. In addition, these cultural products would be relevant to other populations both displaced and struggling under global capitalism. These cultural products, especially music, become important means of cross-cultural communication, a means of expressing issues of politics, place, and identity. Global music becomes "an international dialogue built on the imagination and ingenuity of slum dwellers from around the globe suffering from the effects of the international austerity economy imposed on urban areas by transnational corporations and their con-centrated control over capital" (Lipsitz, 1994, p. 27). In other words, global music is an important cultural resource for youth, like that for which Cindi Katz was arguing in the previous chapter.

Local musicians can speak to local social and political conditions in ways that might resonate elsewhere. For example, South African reggae performer Lucky Dube sings in his song "Prisoner" about the importance of education to avoid becoming a victim of the state. Without education we become literal prisoners, locked up in a bur-geoning prison system. They don't build schools anymore, he sings, only prisons. Given global disinvestment in education and investment in the carceral system, this song has resonance in many places, espe-cially the US, which locks up minority populations (especially black males) in staggering numbers rather than adequately funding urban schools.

Musicians can also speak to the experience of displacement, living in foreign lands, longing for real or imagined homelands. For exam-ple, Ugandan musician Geoffrey Oryema, living in exile in Paris, uses displacement as the main theme of his recordings, as evidenced by CDs titled, *Exile* and *Nomad*. His album *Night to Night* contains a num-ber of ballads full of longing and loss. In the song "At my Window" he expresses his feelings, looking across Paris rooftops, of exile. The track "Sardinia Memories (After Hours)" is a nostalgic recreation of

Kinshasa before Idi Amin, of music and youth, sitting at a bar and listening to Radio Kigali.

And musicians can speak to trans-Atlantic, and transnational, movements of people and music, like that discussed earlier in this chapter. Lipsitz (1994, p. 27) gives the example of "Jamaican toaster Macka B [who] raps an English-language history of Senegal over the singing of Baaba Maal, who speaks the Pulaar language of his native land." But more than just being a cross-cultural collaboration, this recording, "Yelle," points out the similarities between the Senegalese musical form of Yelle and of reggae music, explaining them through the history of Senegal, especially Senegal's role as the departure point for slave ships heading for the Americas.

Global music, then, is far from being placeless music, but, Lipsitz argues, is about place and displacement. It is also a means of speaking not just of politics and place, but identity. It is a means of invoking strategic essentialism and strategic antiessentialism (recall his example of the Mardi Gras Indians in Chapter 1). Popular music is a crossroads not just in terms of sharing communication and experience but a crossroads of identity as well.

However, Lipsitz refers to the crossroads of popular music as *dangerous* crossroads. These practices of identity, for example, run a number of dangers, including the simple perpetuation and reinforcement of egregious racist imagery. What, after all, do Native Americans get from the Mardi Gras Indians' performance? That is, the wearing of disguises, be they literal masks or the taking on of cultural and musical forms (enveloping oneself in a cultural territory of heavy metal, hip hop, or punk, for example) runs the danger of reinforcing the system of cultural and economic inequality that produced these forms or conditions that brought them as commodities to be consumed globally. For musicians, engaging in the global music marketplace has both strategic advantages and risks. The advantages include using already established conduits of transnational communication (the global music industry) to speak about local conditions and to connect and communicate with other aggrieved populations, using international recognition and connections to local political advantage, and so on. For example, the Haitian group Boukman Eksperyans uses their fame to stay alive and out of jail as they sing about oppression by the Haitian government (Lipsitz, 1994). The risks include the following: if the political and economic conditions they are living in and responding to are caused by the exploitation of their country by capitalist transnational corporations, by signing record deals and releasing commercially successful records aren't they participating, in the end, in their own exploitation? And isn't there the danger of turning the pain and struggle of, for example, Haiti or South Africa into just another novelty for the Western middle class to dance to in clubs or to play at dinner parties?

The idea of strategic antiessentialism is a useful one for understanding some of the reasons global musicians may choose to express themselves through global forms. Are Korean youth dressed in hip hop fashions and performing rap songs simply victims of cultural imperialism (chasing the latest global fad)? Or do they choose that form strategically to say things they otherwise wouldn't be able to? Probably a bit of both, sometimes more of one than another. But it is to the taking up of these global forms to which we now turn, reminded of Wilk's notion of the structures of common difference. Common forms allow local musicians to communicate with local musicians elsewhere through a common code. But it also potentially limits the vocabularies of that conversation to the norms and conventions of the form, which were structured elsewhere. In terms of music, heavy metal, hip hop, reggae, punk, and rock have become something of global forms. But so have jazz and Western classical music, the latter of which followed colonial empires across the globe. I wish to focus here on just two forms: punk and hip hop.

Forms of Global Music

Punk

Punk is most commonly considered a music and style from mid-1970s Britain. Punk was a rejection and inversion of mainstream culture. For example, it inverted fashion norms so that torn and soiled clothes were what was worn, and items such as safety pins, chains, and garbage bags became part of the style. Dick Hebdige (1979) argues that punk was a dramatization of British youth's disillusionment with mainstream culture, especially the disconnection, slickness, and commercialization of popular music. The commercial media industry had a voracious appetite for new trends, mining youth culture for a creative jolt. Punk was, in part, a reaction against being assimilated – being as offensive as possible as if daring the media to assimilate them. If pop music was overproduced and prepackaged, punk musicians prided themselves on not being smooth or technically proficient. Punk magazines left in typographical errors and the marks of pasting up the pages.

The origins of punk precede this moment, however. Andy Bennett (2001) emphasizes punk's Do-It-Yourself (DIY) ethos as being central to what is punk, rather than just its style. Make your own clothes, your own magazines, your own music. He then places the origin of the punk ethos in the US garage bands of the 1960s, bands making music in their own spaces, their own way – anyone could start up a band. This punk ethos was revived in New York a few years later with a focus on pared down music and small scale venues – a reaction to the rise of large-scale stadium rock and the overly elaborate and pretentious art rock. Producer Malcolm McLaren visited New York at this time and, impressed by what he saw, returned to London and created a London punk rock group, The Sex Pistols. The UK punk movement was, therefore, not just a youth movement but closely associated with commercial ventures and art schools. As a style, UK punk tends to be much more aggressive and chaotic than New York punk.

As punk travels it is important to note that it does not do so in a general or abstract way. Lines of communication and influence are specific, historical, and unequal in terms of direction of flow and access (O'Connor, 2002, 2004). Tours by punk bands are influential in spreading punk style, as are distribution networks via local punk or alternative record stores circulating records, CDs, and tapes as well as fanzines. Internet access has been useful for the Mexico City punk scene (O'Connor, 2004) and virtually essential for the South Korean punk scene (Epstein, 2000). Limitations on flows are placed by economics (affording the music) and language. For example, the US punk industry (a contradiction in terms that it is, "punk industry") has the economic power to distribute globally, but punks in other countries, especially poorer countries like Mexico, can't afford to return the favor and so are virtually unknown in the US. Language proves a barrier as well, as Spanish language punk doesn't travel well in US punk circles.

Rather than being a global form imposed on local musicians from afar, with local punks providing pale imitations of Western acts, Alan O'Connor argues that punk is taken up according to local needs and differentiates according to local conditions. He turns to the notion of habitus as a way of explaining the social structures that allow and limit the possibilities of a local scene. Here he emphasizes the structuring nature of habitus more than we did in Chapter 1: "Bourdieu's notion of habitus is intended to overcome the idea that, for example, tastes in punk music are completely a matter of individual choice or that there is such a thing as 'Mexican punk' or 'Spanish punk'" (O'Connor, 2004, p. 178). Later he writes: "In the dialectic between individual tastes in music and what is easily available, there is a structuring structure: on the one hand, the social organization of musical tastes; and, on the other, the distribution channels for punk music" (p. 179).

As we have been discussing throughout, territorialization is not simply a voluntarist effort, but one structured by history and social conditions. We territorialize, but not on a blank slate, not in territories of our own making. Therefore, "punk subculture is selectively accepted in Mexico according to the needs of marginalized Mexican youth" (p. 178).

A punk scene is then dependent on a number of structuring factors: availability of places to play, practice, and live; size and commitment of audiences; and so on (O'Connor, 2002). For example, the punk scene in Mexico City described by O'Connor is a politically colored lower working class phenomenon organized around punk collectives. He estimates that there are about 5,000 punks in Mexico City and two to three punk shows a week. Lack of resources is a crucial structuring principle. Social justice is a key theme of punk shows; and there is a deep suspicion of the commercial music industry and any notion of profit. Mexican or international punk bands who have signed contracts are rejected by the Mexico City punk scene. Music is distributed via cassette rather than records or CDs, and concerts don't occur in clubs or bars (too expensive) but in available public spaces like basketball courts in working class neighborhoods. Punk shows start and end early so that the audience, reliant on public transportation, can scatter back across the city via long bus rides. Instrumentation is limited because of the expense of instruments, which are also shared among groups, and the music is structured and mixed so that the political lyrics can be clearly heard. The political dimension of punk clearly dominates here.

O'Connor contrasts this scene with the punk scene in Barcelona, Spain, where there are networks of more established squats and community resource centers which punks share with other groups. Whereas in Mexico punk political commitments are via the collective (that is, one's politics are the politics of the collective), politics in Spain is more individual (that is, one's politics are one's own choice, not determined by the collective). There are also a number of community radio stations, giving punks greater access to the airwaves than they have in Mexico City, and a number of punk record stores. In Mexico City music is exchanged in the El Chopo market rather than through stores. All these point to very different economic circumstances in Barcelona and Mexico City, very different political support for social issues and services. Punk shows in Spain tend to be much smaller with a greater variety of musical styles (from politics to parody) and style of dress (which tends to be more subdued than the Mexican punks).

Both of these punk scenes differ markedly from the punk scene in Indonesia described by Emma Baulch (2002) where rock music, especially heavy metal (Metallica), alternative rock (Sonic Youth), and mainstream punk (Green Day) became the domain of newly wealthy middle class youth in the 1990s.[3] A combination of alternative and punk (alternapunk) became associated with what Baulch called a "metropolitan superculture." Out in the peripheral regions of Indonesia, however, the situation was more complex. Bali, for example, is struggling to maintain a sense of regional cultural identity in the face of encroaching globalization and modernization – exemplified by the growing tourist industry, the establishment of shopping malls, and the growth of a deregulated media industry. Baulch argues that Bali is not responding to a generalized global other, but to globalization funneled through the metropolitan capital, Jakarta. Their cultural struggle is then not Bali versus the world (or the West), but Bali versus Jakarta.

In the mid-1990s a number of local alternapunk bands formed in Bali, inspired by images of a Green Day concert in the capital of Jakarta and corresponding radio play of Green Day songs and TV broadcast of Green Day videos. These bands were seen locally as sellouts to metropolitan culture – pale imitators of foreign bands, rejecting local Balinese identity, etc. To cap it off, these bands tended to hang out in the malls, the übernonplaces of globalization. These bands were also seen as sellouts by local reggae and deathmetal groups who saw *themselves* as the authentic youth culture of Bali standing in opposition to homogenizing globalization. The deathmetal groups even incorporated local cultural themes and languages into their original compositions (which the alternapunks did not). All these groups, alternapunk, reggae, and deathmetal, were based in foreign musical forms, only the reggae and deathmetal stood in opposition to the metropolitan (despite the fact that the reggae groups tended to play mainly at the tourist resorts), while the alternapunks embraced the metropolitan. The alternapunk groups did not see themselves as sellouts, obviously, but positioned themselves in a liminal space. In particular they saw their choice of music as a rejection of the pressure to adhere to a conservative local cultural identity. They saw themselves as truly alternative (though they thought that most local youth just didn't get it yet). In identifying with the metropolitan center they were not identifying with the foreign global other, but with what they saw as an authentic site of alternative culture, a source of cultural *disorder*.

> The anti-authority message and the invitation to disorderliness underlying the medium – "alternative/underground" and rock music in New Order Indonesia more generally – may well have been more important than the verbal discourse of the songs. Disorder, always the political antithesis of the New Order, became "in" for the younger generation. (Sen and Hill, 2004, p. 82)

It was this cultural disorder, this cultural nonplace, this space of freedom, that the alternapunks sought, bit by bit, to establish in Bali.

> It is not so much *what* the songs say, but how they go about presenting it, and the whole sensual environment which rejects repression and supports anarchy. With the assistance of a punk ethos many Balinese young people are creating an environment which assists them to cope with their culture in a world which is becoming more and more stifling as the pressure to please Western tourists grows. (Laskewicz, 2004, p. 195)

Thus, when an underground countercultural punk movement finally formed in Bali in the late 1990s, they looked back to these alternapunk bands as their origin and not the reggae or deathmetal bands who had dismissed them as global fashion victims and cultural pollutants (Baulch, 2002).

In Seoul, Korea, the local punk scene was, likewise, inspired by imported alternative (Nirvana) and punk (Green Day). Because of the Korean economic boom of the 1980s and the rise of a new generation of youth, discussed in the previous chapter, youth were familiar with Western popular music style and fashion through travel and the consumption of imported CDs and media images. Hip hop style became especially popular. In 1992 an underground rock performer, Seo Taiji and the Boys, released Korea's first home-grown rap CD, which proved revolutionary (Howard, 2002; Morelli, 2001). Not only was the CD phenomenally popular, the group inspired a hip hop fashion craze and changed the Korean music industry in the process. Before Seo Taiji's CD, over half of the Korean music market went to foreign releases (Russell, 2003). Seo Taiji helped open a creative space where local artists could experiment with a variety of styles (rap, rock, alternative, punk) and be met with success. By the mid-1990s local acts were dominating the Korean market. There was a feeling that Korean bands could create their own sounds, their own rap, rock, and punk. This sense of self-empowerment resonates strongly with the philosophy behind the Haja center discussed in the previous chapter: Let's do it! This DIY movement in the realm of local music also enabled the creation of a Korean punk scene, dubbed Chosôn Punk. Hongik University in Seoul is known for its arts school and the area around Hongik, Hongdae, became one of the new cultural zones, reterritorialized by the new generation (like Apgujungdong). Hongdae became the place, through a variety of clubs, where audiences and bands could experiment with different styles. In general, the Hongdae music scene(s) was an alternative and non-commercial space (Lee, 2006).

In 1994–5 the first bands began appropriating elements of punk (Epstein, 2000). The most prominent club for punk was a place called "Drug" in Hongdae. In 1996 Drug began releasing its own CDs, beginning with the first punk compilation, *Our Nation, Volume 1*. The most successful of the Chosôn Punk bands to come out of Drug is Crying

Nut. Crying Nut was formed in 1995 by a group of high school friends. Crying Nut is a band proficient with classic punk riffs, infused with a sense of fun and energy, and rapidly diversifying its musical spectrum – including ska, heavy metal, Irish folk, and others, but "with Korean feeling" (Hau, 2001). The band winks at the Koreanization of punk in titling a track "Myungdong Calling"; the title an obvious echo of the Clash's classic punk song, "London Calling." They have a punk cover version, sung in Korean, of "Over the Rainbow" which, frankly, rocks. In 2001 they produced and starred in an independent film, *Looking for Bruce Lee*. Crying Nut is probably the only punk band in the world to have gone on a three year hiatus so band members could complete their country's compulsory military service. In 2006 they reformed, released their fifth album, *The Cow of OK Pasture*, and toured the US. Their commercial success in punk terms is problematic and they refer to themselves as "imitation punks" (Epstein, 2000, and n.d.). Though they and their music can be heard in commercials, their success is primarily due to a grueling tour schedule rather than extensive airplay.

Punk in Korea tends more towards an aesthetic and ethical punk and less towards politics. Theirs is not a class rebellion, and, indeed, Chosôn Punk is primarily a middle class phenomenon, a product of the new "spoiled" generation discussed in the previous chapter (see Yi, 2002). And though it maintains its DIY and underground ethos, its primary target of critique is not consumer culture. Rather, like mainstream US punk like Green Day or alternative bands like Nirvana, Chosôn Punk concerns itself primarily with middle class alienation and boredom. They sing about the problems and pressures of the education system and the demands of parents who don't understand. As Stephen Epstein (2000) describes in his overview of the scene,[4] the key themes of Chosôn Punk songs are desire for freedom, the relief from stress, and a sense of discontent. These songs are couched as personal narratives about the everyday, rather than as broad-based critiques of culture or politics. Korea is not unfamiliar with political popular music, which was prominent during the student uprisings of the 1980s. But Chosôn Punk tends to be a rejection of political rock and remains "an aesthetic counterculture" (Epstein, 2000). What the punk scene, and more broadly the Hongdae scene, provide is a space of release, of freedom from everyday life. These are spaces where youth of high school and college age can go to blow off steam, play a bit with identity, and find others to relate to. These are spaces of affective alliances of collegiality and collectivity (Lee, 2006). More significantly, these spaces are seen as *Korean* spaces filled with their own kinds of rap, punk, or heavy metal. There is a repeated insistence by bands and fans that there is something Korean happening here. Reflecting on the incorporation of rap, reggae, house, and other musical forms into Korean popular music in the wake of Seo Taiji, Keith Howard (2002, p. 90) writes:

> Although Korean audiences may initially have been attracted to the new music precisely because the appropriated styles were foreign in origin, the process of acculturation turned the foreign into a vernacular expression. While the stylistic origins of the new music may have been foreign, its content was clearly Korean, tied to an aesthetic of common experience . . . and discussed within a nationalistic discourse that maintains Koreans constitute a single homogeneous race. The music was something special to the consumers, part of the shared identity of being Korean.

Within Chosôn Punk, an idea of nation is embraced, but as Epstein points out, it is a claim to a nation that the youth themselves have created. When punk compilations are named "Our Nation" this is not patriotism (even ironic patriotism), but a gesture towards a more inclusive sense of nation. When South Korea speaks of itself in political terms it uses the word "Hanguk." But this is *Chosôn* Punk and not Hanguk Punk, and Chosôn gestures back to a unified Korea, not just in political but ethnic and cultural terms (Epstein, 2000, 2001).

Hip Hop

The global influence of hip hop has been traced more comprehensively than that of punk (Lipsitz, 1994, Mitchell, 2001a). Lipsitz (1994, p. 36) has written that:

> Hip hop expresses a form of politics perfectly suited to the postcolonial era. It brings a community into being through performance, and it maps out real and imagined relations between people that speak to the realities of displacement, disillusion, and despair created by the austerity economy of post-industrial capitalism.

Hip hop challenges Western notions of music and music production. Its focus on rhythm means that it is concerned more with, as jazz performer Max Roach has put it, "the world of sound – not the world of music" (quoted in Lipsitz, 1994, p. 37). And it challenges ideas of music production in a number of ways: it turns music consumers into music producers (a machine of musical playback, the record turntable, becomes a machine of musical creation); and it builds its sound out of snippets, samples, of other songs. In this way any rap song is the work of many and not just one author (the DJ) and it relies on the audience's own knowledge of popular music to make the links between the samples (Lipsitz, 1994; Rose, 1994).

Significantly, hip hop is associated not only with Black culture but Black politics – from the politics which inform the conditions of everyday life for many African-Americans to the politics of Black Nationalism and Afrocentrism (Bennett, 2001). The global dimensions of hip hop, therefore, emphasize its effects on and origins in African diasporic populations. We should note that the dominant description of hip hop as a purely Black cultural expression is a form of strategic essentialism. On the one hand this move makes hip hop a form of great cultural power for a disenfranchised group, but on the other it ignores the Puerto Ricans and others involved in the early New York hip hop scene and Latino hip hop artists in New York and Los Angeles (Flores, 1994; Mitchell, 2001a). But this is not to downplay the tremendous importance that hip hop has had for African Americans as a means of creating and becoming part of a transnational movement and collective, a transnational dialogue speaking to local political and economic conditions and providing cultural resources for local populations to find a voice and means of expression.

> The ability to find that identity of passions and turn it into a diasporic conversation informing political struggles in similar but not identical circumstances has enabled peoples of African descent to survive over the centuries; it may now also hold the key to survival for the rest of the world as well. (Lipsitz, 1994, p. 331)

Lipsitz points out, however, that "the radical nature of hip hop comes less from its origins than from its uses" (p. 37). As rap records and videos circulate around the globe, hip hop has become an important resource used by a variety of audiences not of African descent. As Tricia Rose (1994, p. 19) notes:

> Rap's ability to draw the attention of the nation, to attract crowds around the world in places where English is rarely spoken are fascinating elements of rap's social power. Unfortunately, some of this power is linked to US-based cultural imperialism in that rappers benefit from the disproportionate exposure of US artists around the world facilitated by music industry marketing muscle. However, rap also draws international audiences because it is a powerful conglomeration of voices from the margins of American society speaking about the terms of that position. Rap music, like many powerful black cultural forms before it, resonates for people from vast and diverse backgrounds. . . . Rap's global industry-orchestrated (but not industry-created) presence illustrates the power of the language of rap and the salience of the stories of oppression and creative resistance its music and lyrics tell.

What's important about hip hop as a form is that it rarely remains as mere imitation but incorporates local cultural, economic, and political conditions. As Tony Mitchell (2001a) has put it, hip hop globally seeks out local roots. Rap music in particular has always been about particular places and spaces, marking territories, providing shout-outs to neighborhoods, streets, zip codes. "Rap artists draw inspiration from their regional affiliations as well as from a keen sense of what [Murray Forman calls] the *extreme local,* upon which they base their constructions of spatial imagery (Forman, 2002, p. xvii, emphasis in original). It is crucial then not to dismiss global rap as mere imitation or just a further example of cultural imperialism. For some, rap music is a means of distancing oneself from, challenging, and irritating the hell out of one's parent's culture. But if this were its only use, it would not continue to be the useful and lasting resource it has become (Bennett, 2001). "[I]t has become a vehicle for global youth affiliations and a tool for reworking local identity" (Mitchell, 2001a, pp. 1–2). It "can be used as a means of engaging with and expressing dissatisfaction at the more restrictive features of everyday life in globally diffuse social settings" (Bennett, 2001, p. 89). We've seen this in effect in our brief discussion of the film *La Haine* in Chapter 3. Rap music has aided a resurgence in *locally* produced music in Korea (as we just saw), a resurgence noted across the globe (Mitchell, 2001a,

p. 32). US rap may have been the inspiration, the spark, but as Mitchell (2001a, p. 12) notes, referencing the hip hop scene in Japan: "the local hip-hop scene caught fire on fuel that was already there." In the survey Mitchell compiled of rap and hip hop scenes outside the US, rap has emphasized local languages (e.g., in the Basque region of Spain), and dialects (in Italy), and cultural practices (e.g., among the Maori in Aotearoa). Far from being limited to themes of youthful angst (as it tends to be in Japan and Korea), rap has also spoken of, spoken within, and supported Basque separatism in Spain, Italian Marxism, the Turkish immigrant experience in Germany, Islamic culture in England and France, anti-racist campaigns in the UK, indigenous rights in New Zealand, and multicultural identities in Australia. Rap groups have also espoused racism, homophobia, misogyny, violence, and narrow-minded ethnic nationalisms – it is not always an instrument of diversity and progressive politics.

Hip hop demonstrates the various and particular flows of people, music, and politics we've been discussing as crucial to understanding cultural globalization. For example, take the South Korean rap group Drunken Tiger who have been influential on the Korean hip hop scene since their first release in 1999. They proclaim that they're on a mission to bring "real" hip hop to the pop-oriented Korean market and even opened a hip hop club in Apgujungdong. They rap in Korean and English and sample Korean music in their work, and their albums are on a Korean label. The group itself, however, formed in Los Angeles and tends to record there. They are on the forefront of an emergence of Korean rappers in Los Angeles. Historically, there have been extreme tensions between the Korean and African-American communities in LA (which came out in the violence of the 1992 LA riots), so the acceptance of Korean rappers in the black hip hop community represents a possibility of reconciliation and dialog between the communities (Prengaman, 2007). Drunken Tiger is basically a rap duo featuring Tiger JK (born in Korea, raised in Los Angeles) and DJ Shine (born in New York but a Korean national; he left the group in 2005), but has also included DJ Jhig (a Korean), Mickie Eyes (a Korean-Italian from California), and Rosco Umali (a Filipino national with a degree from UCLA). Both Tiger JK and DJ Shine's first language is English and their albums show their progression as they refine what Korean they know. In their songs they emphasize their authenticity, their roots DJ-ing in the LA, New York, and Chicago scenes. On the opening track of their third album, *The Legend of . . .*, "WORD," DJ Shine raps, "I'm old school, I've been doing this since the 80s."[5] The Korean public has been receptive to their music, but also somewhat suspicious, since these are "foreign" Koreans. The example of Drunken Tiger highlights the global mobility of young Koreans, and the influence of diasporic Koreans on Korean culture, and asks us to raise questions about any claims to nationality of music, but it also points to the transnational links that hip hop makes available, for example between Los Angeles and Seoul. Drunken Tiger is also a founding member of a transnational collective of Korean hip hop artists called Movement.

If in some ways Drunken Tiger illustrates a transnational take on hip hop, an example of the local roots of hip hop is that of Hong Kong rap group, LMF. To understand LMF's impact, we need to establish something about the context of Hong Kong. Hong Kong was a small fishing village before the British started using its natural harbor to land its opium ships in the 1820s. After two Opium Wars with China, Britain laid claim to Hong Kong island and the adjacent Kowloon peninsula. In 1889 this region was leased to Britain for 99 years. Hong Kong served as a free port under British rule and grew rapidly. Occupied by the Japanese during WWII, Britain reclaimed Hong Kong in 1945. In addition to the port and its trade Hong Kong became a manufacturing and financial center. In 1997 Hong Kong returned to Chinese rule as a Special Administrative Region under the principle of "one country, two systems" which meant that it could remain capitalist and relatively autonomous from communist China.

Writing about Hong Kong, cultural studies scholar John Erni (2001, p. 391) argues: "involves a triangular articulation of Chinese nationalism, British colonialism, and globalism." Communication scholar Eric Ma has argued (2002a, p. 187) that Hong Kong as a British colony had no strong "nationalist imperatives." Hong Kong was a society of immigrants and transients and so did not have strong Chinese or British national sentiments or even a strong sense of local identity (Chu, 2006). The collective identity of Hong Kong was formed through popular culture and it had a strong local culture industry which was regionally influential.[6] But that pop culture industry, especially the music industry, allowed very little independence on the part of the artist

– almost all aspects of the industry were carefully controlled by the corporations. In terms of music, an artist's image, songs, venue, and even name is controlled by the record company. Still, citizens of Hong Kong upheld the sophistication and polish of local media products, such as cantopop songs, and even later in the 1990s turned to the equally polished Japanese pop culture (J-pop), to maintain a cultural distinction from mainland China, which those in Hong Kong considered provincial.[7] All this worked well during the economic boom of the 1980s and 1990s – where a clear Hong Kong identity of cosmopolitan sophistication, undergirded by an ethos of hard work and a belief in upward mobility, seemed to match the reality of everyday life for most. This identity was challenged in 1997 on two fronts: Hong Kong became part of the People's Republic of China, and Asia went through an economic crisis. Cosmopolitan Hong Kong was now Chinese and the myth of prosperity and advancement was beginning to ring hollow for many.

Against this backdrop, LMF released their first EP in 1999. LMF is not really a rap group, but more of a collective "of local underground rappers, graffiti artists, film actors, DJ's and heavy metal guitarists" (Khiun, 2006, p. 62). This was an all-star band of the alternative Hong Kong scene. They first came together for a concert in 1992 but then members spent most of the 1990s on various other projects like the heavy metal group Anodize. What seems to hold the collective together is a shared interest in alternative culture, a DIY ethos, and the ethic of being lazy, that is, being a slacker. To take this last point first, the group responds to the high expectations and pressures of Hong Kong life (hard work and success in education and business) by valorizing the slacker lifestyle. LMF stands for LazyMuthaFucka, a name which began as an in-group joke, a reference to one original band member who they claimed was a "lazy mother-fucker" (Ma, 2002a, p. 189). The collective is also referred to as the Lazy Clan or LMFamily. As Ma discovered in his ethnographic research on the group, most of the members of LMF are not from the elite of Hong Kong society, indeed many would be considered failures by Hong Kong's high expectations, school drop-outs without steady job prospects. Some members are employed full time (at least one has a Master's Degree), but many do freelance work in CD shops, construction sites, delivery jobs, or teach music lessons to get by. Most work hard enough to maintain a basic standard of living, but they prefer when possible to spend time hanging out in the group's band room, playing hobbies (rebuilding CO_2 guns, making models, working on bicycles which they ride late at night through the city). This emphasizes the ethic of DIY. One group hawked meatballs from a cart that they had built, one publishes a 'zine, and so on (Ma, 2002a, p. 192). Most importantly, however, is that they self-produce their own CDs. Their first EP was completely self-financed and distributed, which was just as well since the mainstream music industry wouldn't touch it. Not only did the EP conflict aesthetically with the Hong Kong pop music scene, but they explicitly attack the Hong Kong music industry for its focus on sales rather than quality, and the self-congratulatory nature of its awards ceremonies (for example, in their song "La Na La") (Chan, n.d.). They also attack the media more generally for being sensationalistic and unethical (in the song "Uknuwudafuckimsayin"). This song also points to one of the distinguishing characteristics of LMF's music, the unprecedented number of expletives that riddle their lyrics (Khiun, 2006). Obscenity is part of their attack on Hong Kong society and the media.

LMF are also distinguished by their focus on themes of urban alienation and social issues (Khiun, 2006). They speak out against corruption in the Hong Kong government, the popular subcultural attraction to the notorious Hong Kong gangs, the Triads, and poke fun at how Hong Kong tries to reinvent itself for the world stage. But though they do tackle such issues, their politics tends to be the micropolitics of everyday life rather than a broader macropolitics. They are alternative, but not necessarily subversive (Ma, 2002a). But though they point to various other social problems (from absent fathers to teenage pregnancy to social pressures to succeed) they remain in some ways traditionalists – believing in family values, taking pride in Chinese identity, and so on (Khiun, 2006). LMF's music, videos, and everyday culture is hyper-masculine and patriarchal, depicting women as sexual objects and denigrating "ugly women" (Chan, n.d.). Ma (2002a) argues that such masculine posturing may be a way of compensating for the members' lack of social and economic status.

But Ma also argues that what is important about LMF isn't necessarily the politics of their lyrics but the spaces that they create. These spaces are emotional spaces and alternative ones. Ma reports that LMF's lyrics are unintelligible in concert, screamed over the band and audience. But the power of the vocals and performance creates an emotional space which brings the band and its audience together to express something likewise unintelligible, a rage or frustration or something else which expresses their daily affective experience of life in Hong Kong.[8] The band also creates and maintains a sense of group identity and belonging by using the emotional reaction of Hong Kong culture to LMF and its members (covered in tattoos and other markers of alterity), usually fear and hatred, to territorialize themselves. "They discursively mobilize oppressive energies of social stigmas thrown upon them, turn them around and use these stigmas as their own identity resources for drawing boundaries of inclusion and exclusion" (Ma, 2002a, p. 190).

They also create other territories and spaces of their own. Their (by now near-mythical) band room, called *a.room*, is in an undistinguished old apartment building. Nondescript from the outside, the apartment – a former home of opium dealers and gambling – has been remodeled, rewired, and decorated by the members themselves. The space is territorialized using a variety of local and foreign resources.

> The irony is that the lifeworld of my informants is saturated with foreign cultural elements and yet they are producing very localized spaces and styles with "alien" resources. In the midst of a Hong Kong-style old building in Mongkok, LMF have built their own band room and peppered it with Japanese and American plastic figures, imported instruments and piles of western albums. (Ma, 2002b, p. 138)

And later he writes:

> This translocal space is carved out in a very localized city space, from which domestic life histories have been structured in a DIY fashion. Those translocal elements are used by local bands to empower themselves and their fans to overcome a localized problem they face in Hong Kong. (Ma, 2002b, p. 138)

a.room is a unique space in some respects, but it has strong resonances with other alternative spaces across Hong Kong, for example record shops. *a.room* however is heterogeneous in that it "is simultaneously a space of work and play, a space of home and outside home. . . . *a.room* has become a multiplex of home, studio, playground, meeting place, classroom, and band room" (Ma, 2002b, p. 141).

LMF retained their alternative spaces and practices despite commercial success. Their debut EP sold enough to finally get the record industry's attention and they signed a contract with Warner music. They collaborated with Hong Kong stars, and appeared in TV commercials; they had a line of action figures and MTV even broadcast from *a.room*. Had they sold out? Their trademark obscenity-saturated lyrics diminished in later releases. Ma argues that LMF use their fame and media access tactically. They may headline a commercially-sponsored media event, but they will lead the crowd at these events in chants of "fuck the media!" They create an alternative emotional and symbolic space within the space of commercial media. Of course, commercial media companies love this because it gives them street cred, increases sales, and mines the alternative scenes for their creativity. And once the commercial support ended, the band broke up in 2003 (Lin, 2006). LMF's position, then, is complex and contradictory.

We've seen throughout this chapter how music is used as a territorializing force – whether this be the imposition of foreign territories or the creation of new spaces locally and translocally from which artists and audiences can express. Cultural territorialization can be heterogeneous, contradictory, liberating, and oppressive – often at once, or in turn, situationally. The examination of global music reveals the flows and organization of media, people, finance, ideas, styles, and forms, and how people use these forms as resources to communicate or even just to get by from day to day. We turn now to the creation and rearticulation of new territories, allowing for new possibilities of identity in a globalized world.

Notes

1 As music scholar Reebee Garofalo (1992, p. 4) has noted, "If his [Simon's] purpose was to showcase black South African music, one has to wonder why he named the project after the estate of the white North American who captured the rock 'n' roll crown by employing – some would say imitating – African-American musical styles."

2 On the *Graceland* controversy, see also Feld (1994) and Garofalo (1992). As Garofalo (1992, p. 4) concludes: "Still, the point to be made is that, for all its flaws, *Graceland* cannot be neatly contained within a formulation like cultural imperialism. On balance, its effect has been progressive."

3 For background, see Krishna Sen and David T. Hill (2004) who set out the various historical and political dimensions of Indonesia's popular music, describing both the national popular Dangdut music (with its roots in Indian film songs) and various underground music scenes, both in relation to Indonesia's long-term military regime dubbed the New Order. On pop music in Bali more specifically, see Laskewicz (2004).

4 As this book went to press, I discovered that Stephen Epstein and Timothy Tangherlini had produced a documentary on the Chosôn Punk scene in 2001, *Our Nation: A Korean Punk Rock Community*, the existence of which had successfully eluded me these past six years (so it goes). The documentary follows a number of punk bands, including Crying Nut and an all-female group, Supermarket, and features interviews with fans and scholars, including cultural studies scholar Cho Han Haejoang (see Yi, 2002).

5 In quoting this, I am not being ironic here and do not mean to imply that Drunken Tiger are somehow inauthentic (e.g., how can they be old school if they are Korean?). Hip hop clearly was the formative culture of the band members, the sounds, styles, practices, and attitudes which surrounded them growing up and with which they territorialize.

6 See Yiu Wai Chu's (2006) exploration of Hong Kong cantopop, discussing "how cultural identity can be made by popular culture" (p. 33).

7 Hong Kong's embrace of Japanese popular music has been an on-again, off-again affair since the 1970s (Ogawa, 2001).

8 In a parallel example, Sen and Hill (2004, p. 85) point out that public concerts in Indonesia had more political impact than oppositional recordings because of this affective dimension. "The undirected communal passions of live concerts, much more than even the most politicized lyrics on the recordings, seemed to represent both the threat and the promise for the New Order state." Popular concerts were used to mobilize both opposition to and support for the New Order regime.

5

Territories of Cultural Globalization

So far in this book we've sketched out some of the cultural processes of everyday life, the ways we move through places and spaces and make spaces our own. Everyday life consists of any number of overlapping territories, some with more salience than others at particular times, some of which we may not have much purchase on or agency in their construction. Spaces and territories precede us, supersede us, make us who we are, and are our legacy. These territories are intimate, local, and global, and the means by which we territorialize can consist of a myriad of signs and markers, each with their own histories and trajectories (some quite global). These signs and markers are deterritorialized and reterritorialized by ourselves, our communities, our media. We've looked at the processes of globalization, the territorializations of and by youth, and how music is an important instrument in territorialization. What I'd like to do in this chapter is provide a number of examples of cultural territorialization that speak to the creation and negotiation of identity. Since we've just been discussing the Asian music scene we'll begin with the example of Chinese pop star Faye Wong's reterritorialization of female identity in Hong Kong and the example of Singapore's Dick Lee who sought to articulate a pan-Asian identity through frothy pop music. Lee's act of territorialization erases borders and ignores particularities in displays of cultural similarity and difference. This exercise in strategic essentialism raises questions about the strategy more generally, a strategy further complicated through a discussion of the example of Panlatinidad in the US and issues of belonging and border crossing.

Next we'll discuss how the diaspora of South Asians to the UK have created a number of spaces for the performance of new identities through the reterritorialization of traditional Punjabi bhangra music. Finally we'll turn to the example of how the diaspora of South Asians to the US raises crucial questions of citizenship and belonging, ideas that undergird this entire book. As they have been throughout this book, the examples used here are meant to be suggestive and not normative, that is they describe how these processes of cultural globalization have occurred at particular times and places, by particular people in certain economic and historical circumstances. These are examples of strategies meant to provoke further thought and discussion rather than be taken to be exhaustive or representative.

Faye Wong

Recall what we said in Chapter 4 about the Hong Kong music scene – it is trendy, fashion conscious, and superficial. Acts are created and directed by recording companies that exert total control over an artist's look, songs, and career. In addition, the Hong Kong pop scene is male dominated and women tend to be portrayed traditionally and passively. Hip cosmopolitanism is emphasized to distinguish Hong Kong from mainland China, which is seen as provincial. This divide between Hong Kong and the mainland is further underscored by a linguistic divide: Mandarin is the dominant language of the PRC, while Cantonese is the lingua franca of Hong Kong.

Into this scene, in the late 1980s, came Faye Wong, a talented singer from working class Beijing who immigrated to Hong Kong seeking a performance career (Fung, forthcoming; Fung and Curtin, 2002). To the Hong Kong scene she seemed a provincial hick with a thick Beijing accent – definitely unhip. But her singing talent was recognized and she was given an extreme makeover by a record company – taking the name Wong Chin-Man and the English name Shirley (in itself a common practice for Hong Kong Chinese), learning Cantonese, and portraying traditional Chinese femininity in image and song. Indeed, her first big hit, "Fragile Woman" played out the stereotype of the passive Chinese woman. By the early 1990s her popularity afforded her a certain amount of economic and cultural capital and she began to take control of her own career. The course of the Hong Kong pop music scene is frenetic, with stars releasing multiple albums each year, recording commercials, performing concerts, and often acting in films and TV dramas. So it was unprecedented when Wong took six months off in 1991 and moved to New York to study. When she returned to Hong Kong she brought with her a broader knowledge of music and a taste for the cutting edge. She changed her name back to Wong Fei (or Faye Wong, anglicized), began composing her own songs, singing in Mandarin, and reasserting her identity as mainland Chinese (something her record company had buried in all its promotional materials). Her music also became more avant garde and experimental as she released cover versions of songs by The Cranberries, The Cocteau Twins, Bjork, and Tori Amos. She became outspoken and even criticized the commercialism of the Hong Kong music industry. And she became phenomenally popular.

LMF challenged the Hong Kong system from, at first, outside the system. Wong challenged the system from within and in the process took on not only the control of the music industry but also ethnic stereotypes of mainland Chinese as well as the narrow gender role afforded women. She returned to Beijing and hung out with rock musicians (marrying Beijing rock guitarist Dou Wei in 1996, divorcing him a few years later when he cheated on her), continuing to experiment with musical styles and her personal image, and maintaining an active performing career in Hong Kong and beyond. Her image was further enhanced through starring roles in films, such as Wong Kar-Wai's 1994 film *Chungking Express* and TV series in Hong Kong and Japan. She continued to challenge gender roles in 1997 by giving birth to a daughter and continuing to have a successful career. As media scholars Anthony Fung and Michael Curtin have argued, she provided a new role model for Hong Kong and Chinese youth of a woman who was independent and career-focused on the one hand and who emphasized family values on the other through her devotion to her daughter (recording a song for her in 1998, "You are happy, I am happy," which features her daughter's voice). Faye's appeal is broad-based, but particularly significant to middle class women in Hong Kong, Taiwan, and across greater Chinese society. Fung and Curtin (2002, p. 285) note that "the open interpretation of Faye's persona provides rich symbolic resources that help to mark out a new social terrain for women who have become a significant factor in the work-places and the market economies of Chinese societies." They continue, "[t]he largely unintended outcome of her insistent efforts to craft an image at odds with institutional and cultural conventions is that Faye's ambitions seem to resonate with fans who are negotiating tensions between their own public personae and the traditional expectations of women in Chinese societies" (p. 286).

The example of Faye Wong is important for our study for a number of reasons. Her deliberate, strategic movements back and forth across the cultural and political border between Hong Kong and China questions the relevance of that border and the assumed character of the territories determined by that border. These moves are strategic in that her move to Hong Kong afforded her the career and subsequent cultural and economic capital to move to New York, back to Hong Kong, and to return to Beijing for her cultural comfort while maintaining an active career in Hong Kong and abroad. Her frequent plays with identity and image provide cultural resources to women across greater Chinese society (PRC, Hong Kong, Taiwan, and beyond) and Asian society caught between pressures for economic success, the structures of traditional society, and desire for modernity. This speaks to the location and influence of cultural power as she asserts her influence through the advanced capitalist network of the Asian media industry, which benefits from her sales and creativity.

Dick Lee

Singapore's Dick Lee defies easy description or categorization. Tony Mitchell (2004, p. 96) describes him as "[a] prolific and chameleon pop singer, composer, music producer, choreographer, talk-show host, fashion designer and theatre director." To this we can add talent scout, TV artistic director, and a VP of Artists and Repertory for Sony. Lee is interesting for us here because his work (songs, musicals, performances) embodies a particular cultural hybridity and makes an argument for a pan-Asian identity. However, the strategic essentialism he espouses in his playful lyrics is not wholly a retreat to one essential ethnic identity (e.g., Chinese) or set of pan-Asian values (e.g., Confucianism). Rather he recognizes that all Asians are necessarily both Eastern and Western; that they cannot ignore the ways that they are Western. However, this does not mean that they have to fully embrace the West – Lee espouses a "modernization without Westernization" (Kong, 1996, p. 288). Lee is virtually unknown in the West despite his intentions to rearticulate – reterritorialize – Western perceptions of Asia as much as his intention is to assert a new Asian identity itself.

Significantly, Lee is from Singapore. Singapore, like Hong Kong, is a financial center, a key node on the global finanscape, and center for global trade with one of the busiest ports in the world. And, like Hong Kong, Singapore was essentially founded by the British as a free trade port in the 1820s. Singapore was under the jurisdiction of British India until 1867 and Britain until 1941 when the Japanese occupied it. After WWII, Singapore was reclaimed by Britain but achieved independence in 1959. It was briefly a part of Malaysia but seceded in 1965. It has been argued that Singapore was forcibly separated by the Malaysian government itself since it had nothing culturally in common with the rest of Malaysia. Singapore was founded by the British and populated by an ethnically diverse mix of Chinese, Malays, Indians, and Europeans and so lacked the "indigenous authenticity" of Malaysia (Ang and Stratton, 1997). Lacking a singular dominant ethnic or historical identity, the cultural identity of Singapore has been determined by the government, which is the People's Action Party (PAP) which has been in power since the 1960s. Or, I should say that the cultural identity of Singapore has been subject to a number of determined attempts by the PAP to shape it. For the most part these attempts are based on a concerted effort to avoid any emphasis on ethnic identity and thus avoid ethnic conflict (Wee, 1999).

> In the absence of a pure, native tradition, the PAP embarked on a large-scale program of *inventing* nativity. In a context which was inevitably always-already Westernized, Singapore was determined to turn itself into an authentically Asian nation by celebrating the native origins of the different migrant groups which together make up the population of the city-state. (Ang and Stratton, 1997, p. 58)

But by celebrating this multiracial identity, Ien Ang and Jon Stratton further point out, the Singapore government essentializes each of these groups. Citizens of Singapore are labeled (on their government-issued identity cards no less) as being of one race or another. This policy ignores families of mixed origins (which have to choose a race) and the great diversity within each category. For example, the "Indian" community includes Tamils, Malayalis, Sikhs, Pakastanis, and Sinhalese and the "Chinese" community speaks a number of "mutually incomprehensible dialects" (Singapore, 2007; see also Ang and Stratton, 1997). This practice of racial essentialism and separation actually is carried forward from British colonial practice where it was a means of controlling the population. The multi-racial national identity of Singapore, therefore, relies upon what Wilk would call a structure of common difference. Each race is identified with a particular cultural tradition supposedly brought with them from their homeland. Each population is allowed to be different, but only *culturally*. And they can be culturally different only in ways which do not threaten the unity of Singapore. The essentialized cultural differences are made safe and non-political. So the national identity of Singapore created and promoted by the PAP was based on a particular multiracial identity, but included other aspects as well. For example, early on the idea of Singapore as a modern consumer culture was promoted, but by the 1980s the concept of Confucian modernity became dominant, with an emphasis on "Asian" values (Wee, 1999). National identity then is based not on a common cultural identity but on an explicit *ideology* of shared values such as "nation before community and society above self" and "family as basic unit of society" and so on (see Ang and Stratton, 1997, p. 62). Though the lingua franca of Singapore is English, there are three other official languages: Mandarin Chinese, Malay, and Tamil, though the recognition of these particular languages again ignores the diversity of Singapore's racial groups (one is assigned a "mother tongue" based on one's race, regardless of one's actual heritage or family history). For example, though very few in Singapore (even among the Chinese population) speak Mandarin, a long-term government promotional campaign to *Speak Mandarin* was launched (perhaps with an eye to furthering trade with mainland China (Wee, 1999)). This new campaign (and the emphasis on Confucian values) threatened to create ethnic tensions by promoting Singapore's Chinese population (who make up 75 percent of the overall population of the city-state) over other groups. The cultural identity of Singapore being promoted in the 1990s was a global consumerist modernism with local cultural values. This identity is termed the "new Asia." As Ang and Stratton (1997, pp. 65–6) describe it:

> What is promoted here is an idea of "Asianness" which is both flexible and particularist: flexible in that it can accommodate the consequences of modernization and modernity, but particularist in that this concept of the "new Asian" defines its boundaries through a categorical repression and suppression of the encroachments of Western universalism.

Born in 1956, three years before Singapore's independence, Dick Lee is of Chinese and Malay descent but was brought up in a household and educational system modeled on the British. Growing up Lee thought of himself as "a character in an Enid Blyton novel" (quoted in Kong, 1996, p. 278) and considered himself as English. It was only when he traveled to England as a teenager that he realized that he was different: he was Asian (Kong, 1996). He was always writing music, shaped by Western pop and rock of the 1960s and 1970s and released his first album at age 18, clearly influenced by Elton John, Neil Young, and Joni Mitchell (Mitchell, 2001b, 2004). In his early twenties he studied fashion design in London at "the tail end of the 'punk-rock' boom and the move to 'new romantics'" (Kong, 1996, p. 278). He was influenced by the flamboyant styling and "self-conscious pop ethos" of Duran Duran et al. (Mitchell, 2004, p. 103).

Lee's music freely combined rock and pop forms with selective Asian influences. Tony Mitchell argues that Lee's career can be divided into three phases: the first a period of self-Orientalism, the second a period of "reverse Orientalism celebrating a pan-Asian identity," and the third is his more recent phase of "more nebulously transregional, tropicalist lounge music" (2004, p. 102; see also Mitchell, 2001b). We're concerned with the first two phases here. His early period in the 1980s, after his return from the UK, emphasized pop arrangements and lyrics spoken in rap. He included multiethnic and multinational collaborators and musicians in his recordings. These early recordings include attempts to capture Singapore's hybridity and to begin to wrestle with notions of Asian identity. These songs both play into and parody the PAP's campaign for Singaporean identity. For example, his song "Let's All Speak Mandarin" obviously invokes the government's campaign, but the song is a story about the narrator awkwardly trying to flirt with a Chinese TV actress at a mall, only to have her speak to him in Mandarin, which he doesn't understand. Lee's first attempt to capture Singapore, "Life in the Lion City" (1984) depicts the city as full of tourists and department stores; life is a rush, but work is frustrating; it's a tropical paradise, but it's hot and uncomfortable. The lyrics name local stores, streets, catch phrases and slogans ("Productivity"; "Keep the City Clean"). It's a city the narrator states he will never leave, but it's not a wholehearted celebration either. The second attempt to capture Singapore is the ebullient version of the folk song, "Rasa Sayang" on his breakthrough album, *The Mad Chinaman* (1989). Tony Mitchell described the song as an "easy listening/prog rock/Singlish rap and drum machine/anthemic pop jingle version of a popular Malay song" (2004, pp. 104–5). The song presents a narrative of the founding of Singapore, gesturing to both a legendary Sumatran prince, Sang Nila Utama, who supposedly discovered Singapore, and Sir Stamford Raffles of the British East India Company who founded the city of Singapore as a free trade port in 1819. This combination, a double gesture of East and West, is characteristic of Lee's work. This song is not the presentation of a staid history, however, but is quite playful and irreverent. For example the evocation of Raffles is almost an afterthought, a response to an opening story about the local lions and Utama: rapper Rizal Ahyar asks, "Eh, what about Raffles?" to which the chorus responds: "We love that guy!" After this history the song turns to a discussion of what's great about Singapore today. Number one is food, and the song lists a number of polyethnic dishes. But next to eating is shopping ("We can eat, eat, eat till we drop, drop, drop/Then we all get up and we shop, shop, shop"). Eating, shopping, spending money earned from tourists – the focus is clearly on Singapore as a consumer culture – success is a pager and a cordless phone, making money and marrying Miss Singapore. All of which is punctuated by a chorus of the traditional folk song sung in Malay. The song, in the end, is both an evocation and parody of Singaporean life.

This period also has Lee struggling to articulate an identity. He described his position as that of a banana – white on the inside, yellow on the outside. Rather than see this as a derogatory term (e.g., to not be a true Asian), he uses it as an acknowledgment that the modern Asian is necessarily both Asian and Western – that one's can't dismiss the influence of the West. In his song, "The Mad Chinaman," he sings about trying to find balance between both halves: The Mad Chinaman is both East and West, traditional and international. He picks up on this theme on a later album in a song entitled, "Banana," where he sings about feeling awkward and out of place with this double feeling of being both Eastern and Western. He travels around trying to find a solution but never fits in wherever he goes. Finally he comes to a double realization: first, that he's fine with his identity as a "banana" and stops contesting it, and, second, this condition is prevalent across modern Asia so he's no longer alone. In pursuing these themes in song and image Lee has been described as self-orientalizing, that is of taking on stereotypical Asian images, but also playing with those images. For example, the pictures accompanying the album, *The Mad Chinaman*, present Lee wearing full traditional Chinese opera costume and make-up, but wearing Doc Marten boots.

In the second phase of his work, in the early 1990s, Lee presents an even broader pan-Asian identity. Wee writes that Lee is "the only Asian pop artist I know who directly set out to depict – and, in some abstract sense, to territorialize – the vacant idea of Asia" (1999, p. 112). He does this through a positive evocation of the term "Orientalism" in the album and song of that title. Orientalism, as he defines it in song, is a positive Asian identity that is both East and West. In this effort at strategic essentialism he argues that Asians are all the same in their combination of traditional spirit and modernity (as he sings in his song "Modern Asia"). Considered in these terms the new Asian is no longer a minority but a vibrant majority. The song sketches this new territory by invoking cities. The Orient, according to Lee, encompasses Paris, Tokyo, Dallas, Cairo, Zurich, Hong Kong, Munich, Saigon, New York City, Quezon City, Casablanca, and "Singapura." New Asians aren't stereotypes or tokens. Lee sings: "We simply have to be/assertive, make them see/this is the new Asian/ Ready for the twenty-first century."

The danger of this strategic essentialism is that it ignores the diversity of Asian experience, and uses selective diversity (such as using particular folksongs, instruments, or languages) in a superficial way. Indeed it reduces Asian cultural differences to safe differences such as music, food, dance – a structure of common difference that comports well with global capitalism (Wilk, 1995) and with the Singaporean state's efforts to construct a national identity. It is also unclear just what this pan-Asian identity looks like, though Lee seems to emphasize Chinese traditions and images. It is highly problematic to claim that all Asia is essentially Chinese. And given China's size, growing economic might and influence in the region, one could understand why the claim of a new Asia which is Chinese might not sit well with everyone.

Lee has his share of critics, most of whom criticize his music as overblown, fashionable pop spectacle with little substance (Wee, 1999). But in the end, here is an example of pop music trying to do the unexpected: to say something new about the condition of Asian identity at the end of the twentieth century through music that is kitschy, pop, parodic, and traditional. Lee is, after all, not a politician but a performer and producer of mass entertainment and spectacle.

The examples of Faye Wong and Dick Lee highlight the issues of border crossing, identity formation and strategic essentialism as important for understanding everyday life within cultural globalization. These issues arise at various levels of identity formation, of territorialization – from the personal to the family, community, nation, and region. However, they are articulated differently at each scale, but all eventually intersect at the level of individual biography, be it that of these pop stars or those who listen to their music. The strategies employed by Wong and Lee are certainly not the only options available to them and others, but are illustrative of choices, possibilities, and problematics within cultural globalization. These choices, possibilities, and problematics depend on a number of material and historical factors, which will vary according to time, place, circumstance. Let me give you another example of how these issues have been tackled, in this case in the US. This is the idea of Panlatinidad, a pan-Latin American identity that encompasses a myriad of nationalities, races, and ethnicities.

Panlatinidad

The debates about Latinidad (the state of being Latino/a) concern the creation of a group identity from within the group itself (that is, in response to the imposition of an identity on the group by mainstream US culture.) Part of that debate has to do with the label used to identify the group itself – Latino/a, Hispanic, or something else? We'll deal with the implications of these choices in a moment. But since I want to open this section with a discussion of marketing and demographics, we'll start by using the term most prevalent in these discourses: Hispanic. If we're seeing a few more Hispanics on TV, in films, or on record shelves it's because of a realization by the mainstream (read: Anglo) marketers that Hispanics represent a major new market (and as of 2000 the largest minority group in the US). That is, there is an understanding that there is a certain cultural and social coherence to Hispanics as a group and that group has more and more economic capital. At the forefront of this push to create a new market are not just Anglo marketers but Hispanic marketers themselves. They are not just selling the Hispanic community to mainstream corporations and audiences but selling this community to itself through the creation and expansion of Hispanic media spaces: TV channels, magazines, and other media (see Dávila, 2001). Indeed, the success of Hispanic media have actually led to a *decrease* in Hispanics on mainstream TV and film screens since advertisers seeking Hispanic audiences turn increasingly to Hispanic media (Dávila, 2001, p. 13). The common identity of this group becomes the group as a market. Hispanic marketers emphasize the group's family values, Roman Catholic roots, and consumption patterns. In many ways, Hispanic is made what Wilk called a safe ethnicity: Hispanic means non-threatening, culturally creative, and overall marketable differences in language, art, food, music, and so on. For example, consider *Chicano* culture, which refers to those with ties to a physical and symbolic homeland in the American Southwest called Aztlán. Chicano/a is a safe ethnicity just so long as they don't actually try to make this homeland a reality but just write books and songs about it. The idea of a Hispanic market ignores the more militant movements that rose up defending migrant workers (though César Chávez is invoked as part of a shared cultural heritage). But though this exercise in strategic essentialism gives Hispanics unprecedented economic and cultural clout (which is advantageous) it is also a strategy of containment (argues Arlene Dávila), a selective representation that silences many ostensibly belonging to the group. For example, if Hispanic TV is one space for the creation of a new Hispanic identity, who gets represented there? According to these images, Hispanics are rather white and middle class and any representation that specifies, for example, national origin rapidly reduces those subgroups to stereotypes (all Cubans are this way, all Dominicans are another, and so on), which indicates and emphasizes myriad ingroup hierarchies and divisions (Dávila, 2002).

The question of who represents the group is also raised by the naming of the group itself. "Hispanic" puts the Spanish language and Spanish origins as the key to the group's identity. But not all Hispanics speak Spanish and to many, especially those indigenous to Central and South America, the term invokes the brutalities of Spanish colonialism and asks them to identify with/as their colonizers (to become "Hispanic"). An alternative designation is "Latino/a" which arose during the civil rights era and which focuses on roots in Latin America. Presumably this excludes immigrants from Spain and other non-Latin American Spanish speakers, but not necessarily as Antonio Banderas has been mobilized as a spokesman for Latino groups despite being from Spain (Dávila, 2001). Either way, Hispanic or Latino/a, they are considered to be a coherent group despite not having a common language, race, ethnicity, or even an identifiable set of names (Valdivia, 2004).

A key problem with how the Hispanic/Latino territorialization has been established especially as a media territory, is that the market is seen as a *foreign* market and not a domestic US one (Dávila, 2001, p. 4). Spanish language television in the US is not about being Latino in the US, but is a transnational venture, consisting of imported programming from Latin America. Latin Americans are overrepresented and US Latinos are conspicuously absent (Valdivia, 2004). The Hispanic market is considered a foreign market, emphasizing ties to other countries. This assumption of foreignness supports an equally inaccurate cultural assumption that all Hispanics are recent immigrants with national loyalties elsewhere. They are always asked where they are from, despite the fact that many have lived in the US longer than most Anglos.

Individuals, therefore, have to negotiate their own identity by relating to media representations of Latinos and a general sense of Latinidad, or group identity. The extent to which any individual embraces either the representations or the group identity varies. For example, some English-dominant Latinos have embraced hip hop as a legitimate site of Latinidad, of the expression of Latino identity. "Hip hop and rap served as reflections of their everyday realities, which they conceived in terms of alterity and marginality vis-à-vis mainstream culture" (Dávila, 2002, p. 33). As we saw in Chapter 4, Latinos, especially Puerto Ricans, were involved in the creation of hip hop in New York in the early 1970s (Flores, 1994, 2000). For subsequent generations of New York Puerto Ricans (Nuyoricans) hip hop has been part of daily life. "Second- and third-generation Latinos have simply stretched the boundaries of Latinidad. They refuse to abide by prescribed notions of Latino aesthetics, particularly when these ignore the experiences of young New York Ricans and are posed as disconnected from African American creative practices" (Rivera, 2002, p. 128). In New York, Latino rappers have created their own, recognized, cultural sphere closely allied with hip hop culture in Puerto Rico and the Dominican Republic. But what is often overlooked, Raquel Rivera points out, are those Latino rappers laboring within the hip hop mainstream, rapping in English and posing "the most overt challenges to traditional notions of Latinidad" (2002, p. 129). In other words, this is not a case of strategic antiessentialism, this is not a mask or disguise, but a practice that speaks to the historical confluence and movements of Afro-diasporic peoples through many routes (Rivera, 2002).

Latinidad, or Panlatinidad, becomes another landscape for individuals to negotiate, establishing themselves within or against. One's position *vis-à-vis* this landscape as well as against the contemporary mainstream (Anglo) landscape can change rapidly. Vicki Mayer (2004) gives the example of Argentinian immigrants to the US. Argentina had been seen for years as the economic success story of South America, its citizens seeing themselves as cosmopolitan and highly educated. They considered themselves exceptional, distinct from the rest of Latin America and identify themselves against the idea of Panlatinidad (indeed, they argued that they were practically European). However, a massive economic crisis in 2001 caused Argentina to default on its international loans, the economy went into free fall and unemployment shot up, with half the country falling into poverty. Faced with this crisis, hundreds of thousands of Argentinians sought to emigrate. But whereas the US had welcomed Argentinians in the past, it became difficult to obtain visas and Argentinians were treated with suspicion. "[N]ew immigrant groups become 'Whiter' when they have capital, both economic and social, to advance in a pluralistic society, as opposed to poorer, 'Blacker' immigrant groups that are subject to discipline and surveillance" (Mayer, 2004, p. 121). In short, Argentinians were no longer the exception to Latinidad and they were treated by the US state in the same categorical terms as the rest of Latinidad. Suddenly Argentinians have to negotiate their position in a landscape they never considered themselves a part of:

> Not necessarily identified as "Latinos" either by themselves or other Latinos, Argentinian Americans become Latinos through the governmentality of the state and the subjectification of other US citizens, including Latinos. At the same time, they are nearly completely invisible in a public culture that either ignores them or combines them with other Latino groups that they share little with. (Mayer, 2004, p. 119)

This is an uncomfortable and confusing position to find oneself in.[1]

The presumption of Latino foreignness in both Latino and mainstream media means that not only are questions of bordering (making Latinos a permanent Other in America) made salient in the discourse of Panlatinidad, but the US/Mexico border itself is made a powerful symbolic reference in debates about contemporary US cultural identity (even if many Latinos have nothing to do with Mexico or the border). But a critical focus on Panlatinidad makes it a useful lever for dislodging discourse about the border and highlights ways that the border has become an important cross-cultural space as well as a fantasy used to maintain mythic notions of national identity and security. The US/Mexico border is seen as absolute – it is a fact. There is presumed to be an absolute distinction between each side: the US is not Mexico, Mexico is not the US. This ahistorical sense ignores the historical and political nature of the border, the fact that people were living in the region long before the border was put into place. For example, performance artist Guillermo Gómez-Peña (1991) in his 1988 performance *Border Brujo* seeks to reterritorialize the border. In this performance he goes back to 1847, before the US/Mexico war, before the establishment of the border, when eight Mexican states suddenly found themselves as a part of the US. The Southwest was Mexico long before it was America. Gómez-Peña dreams of a map without borders – that is, without the fiction/fantasy of the border in place one can create new maps. He envisions a Latin American "archipelago," which reaches the Nuyorican barrios of Boston and Manhattan and includes Central American refugees in Alberta and British Columbia. "My dream," he intones, "becomes your nightmare." But this is not a dream – with burgeoning populations not only in urban centers but in rural communities, not only in California, Texas, and the Southwest but through the deep South and up the eastern seaboard, where small town America isn't dealing with recent or transient migrants but second and third-generation Latino residents, Gómez-Peña's map of Latinidad is a reality.

Within a globalized world, communication which speaks to issues of immigration and the border become essential (cf. Lipsitz, 1994). Gómez-Peña is far from alone in addressing issues of the border. For example, Mexican-American musical superstars Los Tigres Del Norte sing about multiple flows across the border and the effects of the border on everyday life. Los Tigres are virtually unknown to Anglo culture, but phenomenally popular in Mexico, Central America, and the American Southwest – selling millions of albums, performing to crowds in excess of 150,000 in Mexico City, and starring in films. Their music, norteño, is based on the jaunty rhythms of polkas and walzes, driven by accordions, and takes the form of corridos, centuries-old traditional ballads which speak to personal narratives, historic events, and braggadocio. Corridos are a means of communication, of passing news, and Los Tigres' music is one of the conduits of communication that speaks to the realities of the border. Their earliest hits were known as narcocorridos in that they sang about the illegal drug trade – songs extolling the exploits of particular smugglers or events. Their song "Pacas de Kilo," for example, is a pure exercise "in narco braggadocio, delivered in the first person and featuring involved wordplay, insider codes, and double entendres" (Wald, 2001, p. 289). Their first hit was "Contrabando y Traicion" ("Smuggling and Betrayal") (1972) which told the fictional story of Emilio and Camelia who smuggle marijuana up from Tijuana to Los Angeles. After the deal is done Emilio announces that he is leaving to join his true love in San Francisco; Camelia "does not take this farewell with good grace" (as Wald puts it, 2001, p. 13) and shoots him, disappearing with the cash. The song was so popular it was later adapted into a series of films.

But the drug trade is not the only traffic Los Tigres sing about. They also have a number of songs about the immigrant experience – "Vivan los Mojados" ("Long Live the Wetbacks") and "La Tumba del Mojado" ("The Wetback's Grave") – the latter of which points out that while foreigners live well in Mexico, the narrator has to sneak across the border to the US to work. "Jaula de Oro" ("Golden Cage") speaks of how Mexican immigrants do find success in the US but at a cost: loss of Mexican culture. The song includes the voice of a young boy (without discernible Mexican accent), complaining about not wanting to go to Mexico. The narrator desires to return to Mexico but is trapped in the US because of work – it's a golden cage, but a cage nonetheless. Most recently they have sung (in "Jose Perez Leon") about the tragedy of border crossing, the death of an immigrant, suffocating in a trailer (Wingett, 2006).

One of their most powerful songs about the border comes off of their 2001 album, *Uniendo Fronteras*. "Somos Mas Americanos" clearly states that "Yo no cruce la frontera/la frontera me cruzo" – I don't cross the border, the border crosses me. He (the narrator) is called an invader, a foreigner, though it's his own land. But who is he? He is a working man who claims a broad syncretic identity: he is Indian, Spanish, Mexican, Latino, Mestizo; "somos de todos colores" (we are of all colors). We are more American, they sing, than the son of the Anglo; they are more American than all the gringos. In other songs Los Tigres protest the reduction of the term "American" to just mean US citizen rather than a citizen of the Americas (Kun, 2005). These songs speak to realities of everyday experience and corridos parallel rap in this way (Wingett, 2006). This form of popular music has even drawn converts from among Chicano punks who see past the musical differences to find others speaking to their lives (Almada, 2006). "The border [is] an audio-spatial territory of performance" a "contact zone" where heterogeneous musics mix and mingle, producing "audiotopias," aural maps of meaning for Mexican immigrants and their descendants (Kun, 2000, p. 6). These musics "serve as vectors of connection and affiliation between distanced and displaced communities" (p. 14).

Audiotopias

We turn next to another audiotopia, another cultural contact zone, one between two immigrant cultural spaces: Afro-Caribbean and South Asian in the UK. The first cultural space is that of sound system culture; the second will be that of bhangra. The end of World War II saw an influx of immigrants from across the British Empire to the UK. Afro-Caribbeans moved in to working class neighborhoods, but were treated with hostility and suspicion by the working class. Banned from the white working class spaces of leisure, such as the pub, Afro-Caribbeans had to establish their own clubs, their own spaces for leisure and for the reaffirmation of community (Back, 1996). Integral in the creation of those spaces was the music of reggae and the establishment of sound systems, cultural forms which they brought with them from the Caribbean.[2] A sound system is like a large portable stereo system that can move from venue to venue. Each sound system has its own technical particulars – sound effects, speaker size, and so on – as well as their own collection of records and MC's who "chat" over the music in particular styles. Sound system events were collective cultural spaces – the DJ and MC carefully reading the crowd and adjusting music selections, and involving the crowd in call and response. Chatting will reference the crowd, calling out individuals, relating recent events, bragging, and so on (Back, 1996). These events provide opportunities for Afro-Caribbeans of multiple national and cultural origins to connect together, to engage in what it means to be Afro-Caribbean in Britain at that time. Les Back (1996, p. 210) writes: "The sound systems establish an entire acoustic environment that transcends any simple notion of playing records. The field of sounds, or soundscape . . . is established within which transnational references can be registered. The dance is about making connection with the denizens of the Black Atlantic." Though reggae style and patois draw on Jamaican geographical and cultural references, the British sound systems make them signify for Britain, applying them to the local context.

"The reggae sound system dances are a predominantly black social constituency" (Back, 1996, p. 211), but other black cultural spaces drew more mixed groups. According to Back, the soul scenes of the 1970s crossed class as well as race and the dancehall scenes of the 1980s were multiracial as well. Whereas reggae sound system culture helped bring together and create a unified Afro-Caribbean community, these other "Black styles operated as a socially cohesive force that unified young people within these alternative spaces. This was particularly profound for young whites who found themselves owning black cultural forms" (Back, 1996, p. 216).

From the other end of the British Empire came immigrants from Bangladesh, India, Pakistan, and Sri Lanka. They too created their own cultural spaces in Britain, in particular in the form of the day-timers – musical events held in the afternoon so young people could attend without breaking curfew or appearing too wild by going out clubbing at night (Bennett, 2001; Back, 1996). The musical form which formed the basis of a collective South Asian identity was derived from Punjabi harvest festival music, *bhangra*. Though specific to a partic-ular region of India and Pakistan, bhangra in the 1980s became the music of the South Asian diaspora in the UK (or at least some sections of it). However, this bhangra was a fusion of traditional Punjabi styles with urban dance music, drum machines, electric guitar and bass, and synthesizers (see Dudrah, 2002). The new bhangra was no longer Punjabi but British, as it was a British invention. In this way it pro-vided one means of establishing a cross-cultural South Asian iden-tity (a British-Asian, or Brasian, identity (Kaur and Kalra, 1996)). Bhangra is not the music of one diaspora (from South Asia) but many, including Afro-Caribbean: "Bhangra, a transnational performance of culture and community, reveals the processes by which *multiple* diasporas intersect both with one another and with the national spaces that they are continuously negotiating and challenging" (Gayatri Gopinath, quoted in Dudrah, 2002, p. 367). Bhangra continues to be phenomenally popular among South Asian audiences, some acts selling over 3 million albums (Burrell, 2003). Though there have been some substantial bhangra influences on mainstream British culture (for example recent soundtracks to films such as *Bend it Like Beckham*, *Monsoon Wedding*, or *Bride and Prejudice* or West End musicals such as *Bombay Dreams*), the market for bhangra itself exists as a separate, self-enclosed entity – driven by small, South Asian music shops, Ian Burrell notes. The CDs and cassettes often aren't part of the database that generates the British pop charts, and many don't even have bar codes so they can't be scanned and sales can't be tracked. They don't appear on the British charts though their sales can exceed those of some mainstream pop artists.

The examples of reggae sound systems and bhangra daytimers shouldn't be seen as "solving" all of the cultural, class, and ethnic conflicts within the strategic essentialisms that are Afro-Caribbean and South Asian identity. They are still a forum for conflict and difference (Bennett, 2001), but they are one means of inter-group and intra-group communication. At the same time, both groups are referred to in Britain as "Black" despite quite different origins and conflict between and within these communities. Both communities are products of and carry the legacy of British colonialism, and both communities have been subject to racism and involved in concerted anti-racist campaigns. But in this broader instance as well popular music can provide a useful resource for cross-cultural dialogue. "Popular music in Britain plays an important role in building solidarity within and across immigrant communities, while at the same time serving as a site for negotiation and contestation between groups" (Lipsitz, 1994, p. 126). The artist most commonly pointed to as providing the connections between Afro-Caribbean and South Asian communities is Steven Kapur, who goes by the name of Apache Indian and whose music synthesizes reggae sound system and bhangra, creating a potential political and cultural alliance through popular song and performance.

Apache Indian

Apache was born to Punjabi parents in Handsworth and went into the family business as a welder. But he grew up in the reggae sound system culture, wore dreadlocks, and identified with reggae and Rastafarianism. He began working on various sound systems, buying his own van to drive sound systems around. The Punjabi community saw his lifestyle as a rejection of their culture, and some even mistook him as Afro-Caribbean. Apache tells the story of going into a store and having the shop owner and customers switch to speaking

Punjabi (presuming that he couldn't speak it), warning each other that Apache could be a thief. In the early 1990s he began chatting, and not just driving, and soon gained a following. He began rapping about problems and issues in the South Asian community, and began chatting in Punjabi as well. This led to him being embraced by the community, who realized that he hadn't rejected their culture after all. Apache began integrating not just themes and language but also bhangra samples. The new style – a combination of bhangra and raggamuffin – was called bhangramuffin. Apache's music created a truly syncretic space of black cultural forms. He gained respect within the South Asian community by integrating bhangra and South Asian themes, and respect in the Afro-Caribbean community by collaborating with recognized reggae artists like Maxi Priest. Apache won a best new reggae artist award in 1991 and recorded in Jamaica at Bob Marley's studio. He chats in a mixture of reggae patois, Punjabi, and English, and his music calls for a unity among the various communities. In his collaboration with Maxi Priest, "Fe Real," he opens by calling out to South Asians in a greeting in Punjabi, to Muslims with a salaam aleikum, and to all who love reggae. Les Back (1995) argues that Apache's music creates a new intermezzo culture, a space in between cultures linked through routes to multiple cultures and constituencies. He describes a concert by Apache and Priest where whites and blacks come together around the common beat of the DJ. At another concert they sing to an Afro-Caribbean audience and get them responding in Punjabi; and at a third they sing to a South Asian audience who are shouting out in patois. Performing in India, Apache has crowds of Hindus, Muslims, and Sikhs singing along in Jamaican patois about racial and religious harmony. Apache himself represents what Back calls a "diasporic triple consciousness": "simultaneously the child of Africa, Asia, and Europe" (1995, p. 141). Apache stated in an interview: "When I really sit down and think about it I am not Jamaican, I am not fully Indian; I am a mixture of everything. I also feel very English" (quoted in Back, 1995, p. 139).

The songs on Apache's first full album, *No Reservations* (1993) include a number which seek to introduce the listener to Indian culture and to teach them Indian customs and vocabulary. "Movie Over India," for example, his first big hit, describes a trip to India to make a film, but in the process teaches counting in Punjabi, the names of relatives (aunt, uncle), and so on. "Come Follow Me" is a sequel of sorts, taking the audience on a tour of Indian cities, and includes additional vocabulary lessons and a list of important historical and cultural figures (Gandhi, Ravi Shankar, Lata Mangeshkar, Rajiv Gandhi, and so on). This song is paralleled in some ways by the song "Magic Carpet" where he chats about flying over the Caribbean, listing islands, cities, land-marks, and streets, detailing the geography of Jamaica (but we don't get a cultural introduction to Jamaica here, like we do to India in his other songs). "Arranged Marriage," a more controversial hit, takes the audience step by step through the process of an arranged marriage. It was controversial in that it's unclear whether Apache is support-ing the tradition or being ironic. On the one hand he chats about wanting his parents to find him a sweet, beautiful, traditional, sub-servient wife from back in Jalandhar, India, who will love him and cook for him traditional Indian food. But he ends the song asking the audience to help him with a problem: what's the best time to tell his girlfriend that he's getting married? In some ways the song was popular with Indian audiences because it mapped the precari-ous position many second-generation Indian immigrant youth find themselves in: trapped between being modern (dating) and being traditional (arranged marriages). To counterbalance the view of the "ideal" Indian woman as being subservient (etc.), Timothy Taylor (1997) points out the importance when interpreting the song of attend-ing to the female backing vocal (sung by Natacha Atlas of Trans-global Underground (Swedenburg, 2001, p. 61)): "I want love, or just a lover/because I can be one or the other." This vocal exhibits a much stronger female agency than that of the rest of the lyrics and acts as a response to the ironic masculine posturing of the main narrative.

Apache's subsequent albums throughout the 1990s saw a certain amount of experimentation with styles. *Make Way for the Indian* (1995) adds rap and soul and stronger bhangra influences to his music. Gone are songs about translation and songs about religion are introduced (for example, "I Pray"). *Wild East* (1998) has Apache collaborating with bhangra artists like Malkit Singh rather than reggae artists like Maxi Priest or Frankie Paul as he had done previously. The album relies much more on the bhangra beat and instrumentation and explores the traditional Indian raags – classical scales. The album is more clearly pitched to its South Asian audience, especially his song

"India" which was in support of his own non-profit charity, The Apache Indian Foundation dedicated to relief for poor children in India. The song invokes an awareness for what's going on "back home." India takes on much more of a central role here in the soundscape of the album. This is less so in his follow-up album, *Karma* (2000), which features a duet with Boy George and which is more ecumenical in its influences and returns to calls for religious harmony. In the song, "Religion," he claims that he respects all religions and can't be a follower of just one religion; he wants to embrace them all: Hinduism, Islam, Sikhism, Rasta, Christianity, and Buddhism are mentioned in the song. He often frames his calls for tolerance and peace in the terms of Rastafarianism – particularly in "I Pray" (an unplugged version of the earlier song is included) and "Calling out to Jah." His most recent album, *Time for Change* (2005) is a much more varied soundscape, repeating half of the songs from *Karma* but adding a number of tracks which mark a return to reggae sound-system roots with the introduction of more sexually-oriented, though not explicit, "slack" lyrics.

We've been discussing the trajectory and varying soundscapes of Apache Indian because his work presents an interesting, shifting audioscape, one which Les Back (1995) has termed (following French philosophers Gilles Deleuze and Félix Guattari (1987)) a rhizomic one. A rhizome is a plant without a central root, but propagates through horizontal runners or shoots. With a rhizome you are always in the middle, never at the start or end. Apache's music is not one that originates in either India or Jamaica, it is instead a series of connections forged through historical circumstance. Back (1995, p. 139) writes: "the types of 'fusion' that Apache's music personifies are not arbitrary. What his music demonstrates is a series of departures, identifications which traverse a number of continents then return and pause at Birmingham's cultural crossroads only to re-depart again." These rhizomic audioscapes provide the possibility of cross-cultural dialogue and understanding and represent a local response to shifting global scapes and networks.

However, these scapes are not entirely unproblematic. Though Apache distances himself from the more controversial elements of some dance hall culture (misogyny, rabid homophobia, and an affinity for guns), he collaborates and identifies with artists who do not distance themselves (Back, 1995, p. 144). There is also his problematic use of Native American references. He named himself after his favorite reggae artist Wild Apache Supercat (who was from Jamaica, of African and East Indian descent). Apache Indian plays the obvious pun Indian (India)/Indian (Native American), making use of Native American allusions in album titles (*No Reservations, Wild East*) and in songs referring occasionally to egregious stereotypical iconography like wigwams, bows and arrows, smoke signals, and chiefs (see "Badd Indian," "Make Way for the Indian"), but makes no substantial cultural connection to Native Americans. The only instance when he does this is when he invokes the reggae trope of identifying with Arawak Indians (for example, in "Fe Real" he refers to himself as Apache Arawak Indian). The Arawak Indians were the indigenous population of Jamaica wiped out by the Europeans. This identification with the Arawaks invokes the repression of indigenous populations by colonialism, which becomes part of reggae's response to injustice – by claiming this history as their own, the Arawaks as part of their identity, reggae artists expand their moral stand against contemporary and historical oppression as they too were victims of colonial aggression.

Media and cultural studies scholar Marie Gillespie points out that Apache Indian and other South Asian performers use of American Indian imagery is also a way of creating a public identity as a "familiar other." She writes (1995, p. 5):

> Eastern "Indianness" connotes, in Britain, an uncomfortable political, imperial history of strife and hatred, as well as a culture of absolute "oriental" difference (Said, 1979). But western Indianness – American or "red" Indianness – connotes, through the tradition of "western" genre films and TV shows (as well as by association with country-and-western music), an altogether more benign antagonism grounded in mutual respect. Impossible, no doubt, in the USA itself, this appropriation of native American style, cross-cut with country style, by public avatars of Asian youth culture in Britain, is indicative of a bid to assimilate to the "west" on terms at least partly of one's own making.

The use of Native American imagery then becomes a type of strategic antiessentialism as performers appropriate and play with the mass-mediated identity of Native Americans in order to both fit in within broader British society (by evoking common texts and images of popular culture) and hold true to a sense of tradition and values from their parents. That is, to balance competing forces of territorialization by borrowing from a third.

Other Asian audiotopias

Much of what has been written about the power of bhangra in the South Asian community (a music and voice of their own) and Apache Indian (especially Back and Lipsitz, but others as well) is perhaps a bit too sanguine in outlook and overlooks not only other divisions within the South Asian community but also other means that South Asians have found to express themselves and respond (culturally and politically) to the culture, social, economic, and historical circumstances they find themselves in. Though bhangra has been instrumental in unifying sections of the South Asian population,[3] and has been an important element in musical syntheses like Apache Indian's work or the music of Bally Sagoo from Coventry (who combines classical Indian film songs with dance beats), not every South Asian musician performs bhangra and not every South Asian listens to bhangra (indeed, it's probably more cool with the youth to be over it (Huq, 1996)). A variety of South Asian-fronted acts emerged in Britain in the 1990s playing a variety of forms of music. Les Back (1995, p. 139) points out that "the diversity of these forms of expression confounds the simple characterization that bhangra is the prime form of expression of south Asian youth culture." Some of these musicians play to predominantly Indian audiences, some predominantly Pakistani audiences, some predominantly white audiences, and so on. And just because members of these groups are South Asian doesn't mean that the music they produce is necessarily South Asian – though critics tend to lump them all together, describing their music in Orientalist cliches (hip hop with spice, or including curry references, for example). Indeed, as these groups territorialize in particular ways they have to fend off forces of reterritorialization that seek to essentialize and exoticize them, framing their work within particular expectations. Let's look first at some of these alternative audioscapes and then at the forces of reterritorialization.

Some groups draw heavily on hip hop as a form of expression. Asian Dub Foundation (ADF) is a collective, which developed from a community youth music project (which echoes the Haja effort in South Korea in some respects) (Sharma, 1996). ADF is not purely a rap group but draw on a number of styles. They struggle to make themselves heard as South Asians, challenging stereotypes (for example, that South Asians aren't cool and can't rap), affirming South Asian identity and political agency against both black and white cultural hegemonies in the UK. Like many of the new South Asian groups such as Hustlers HC and Fun^da^mental, ADF is heavily politicized, involved in national anti-racism campaigns and advocating self-defense against racism (Hutnyk, 1996). They also rap in Bengali as well as English, affirming the particularities of their cultural origins against the implicit and explicit Punjabi of bhangra.

Fun^da^mental is a multiracial band out of Bradford. It's leader, Aki Nawaz (who raps under the name Propa-Gandhi) had been drummer for the 1980s punk band Southern Death Cult (which later became The Cult). Fun^da^mental is one of the most outspoken, political, and controversial of the new groups to arise in the 1990s. It promotes a unity of South Asians and Afro-Caribbeans under the common term "Black" as a response to racism. The group includes both South Asian and Afro-Caribbean members. The group's politics, however, are complex and contradictory. Fun^da^mental draws on a number of political discourses from Gandhi to the Black Panthers (their first album was titled after the Panthers' slogan, "Seize the Time") to the Nation of Islam's Louis Farrakhan. Rather than following any one of these, they use these discourses selectively and strategically to craft a response to their contemporary condition. For example they strategically use both a South Asian inflected Islam (80 percent of all Muslims in the UK are South Asian) and the African-American Nation of Islam but also draw on imagery from global Islamic struggles like the kufiya scarf, a sign of the Palestinian intifada or uprising. But as Ted Swedenburg (2001) points out this is far from an orthodox Islam in that, for example, Nawaz will rap lines of the Koran in Urdu and Arabic, which is not permitted by Islamic orthodoxy. Sanjay Sharma (1996, p. 52) writes that "Fun^da^mental articulates eclectically a kind of militant Islamic-influenced, pro-Black anti-racist identity politics." They frame their anti-racism as a militant self-defense (see, for example, "Dog Tribe"). But as Sharma also notes we shouldn't reduce their politics just to the lyrics (contradictory as they may be, and problematically masculinist at times), but remember the energy of their music, the intensity of their performances. As we noted in our discussion of LMF last chapter, this affective dimension can have important political consequences – in this case capturing a sense of passion and urgency. Nawaz himself points out that he enjoys "going up on the stage to hordes of drunk and drugged-out indie kids and almost terrifying the shit out of them" (quoted in Swedenburg, 2001, p. 62). But in addition we have to consider not just the discourse of the lyrics and the affective dimension of their performance, but the rich aural landscape created by Fun^da^mental. What they produce are dense, rhizomic audioscapes that draw on the voices of historical leaders, and the sounds of Qawwali as well as Indian film music. Through its contradictory politics and creative variety of music sampling and influences, Fun^da^mental is not about articulating a clear identity or position, but opening a chaotic affective space against a racist and oppressive society, calling attention to injustices as they see them. Their most recent album, 2006's *All is War* continues this trend. The album is an impassioned diatribe against imperialism, anti-Islamic fervor, and the US-led invasion of Iraq. Its cover depicts the Statue of Liberty posed, with a hood, like one of the infamous tortured prisoners of the notorious Abu Ghraib prison. Its songs speak of the day that Americans will turn to Muslims to rescue them from the hell they have created for themselves; they compare and contrast Che Guevara and Osama Bin Laden; and they explore the point of view of bombers: a suicide bomber, an arms dealer, and an American weapons scientist. So controversial was the album that their own record company (which Nawaz co-founded) refused to release it and Nawaz had to find alternative means of distribution and manufacture (having to find a factory out of the UK). Members of Parliament called for his arrest and Nawaz himself stated that he expects to be arrested under new anti-terrorism laws (Brown and Torres, 2006).

Other Asian-fronted groups are less extreme than Fun^da^mental and don't just draw on hip hop but also punk (The Voodoo Queens) and other forms, and some are simply too eclectic to categorize (for example, Cornershop, Joi). Also arising in the 1990s were the more elitist territorializations of the "Asian Kool" or "Asian Underground" scene which originated in high-end London clubs such as Outkaste (a club and a music label) or Talvin Singh's Anokha. South Asian influenced music and fashion become trendy with mainstream audiences, the latest trend in bourgeois aural and cultural tourism (see Chapter 4). Though Singh in many ways became the face of Asian Kool his club catered primarily to wealthy white audiences (Ahmad, 2001). In some ways, the post-bhangra Asian Kool simply reinforced the expectations made of South Asians to be exotics. Many groups (including ADF and Cornershop) were lumped in to the Asian Underground label and other acts jumped on the bandwagon, taking on South Asian superficialities.[4] This provoked a vocal response by these other artists. At the intro to a live show, ADF state that they've never been allowed to play the upstairs venue before, probably because they were considered to be part of the Asian "underground" (*Conscious Party*, 1998). And on Joi's album, *We Are Three* a voice intones: "This is not the Asian Underground/This is music." Meanwhile bhangra acts have continued, outselling Talvin Singh, and remain a potent public sphere for British South Asians (Dudrah, 2002). Far from being de-politicized dance music, Dudrah points out that popular British bhangra songs have critiqued, for example, unfair racist taxation.

All of these groups face forces of reterritorialization and containment. They bear, for example, the burden of representation. That is, South Asians are seen so rarely in public culture that each representation unfairly is taken to stand for the entire South Asian community in all its diversity. "All those involved are immediately seen as spokespersons for the 'community' and 'their generation' even if their music is not particularly 'Asian'" (Huq, 1996, p. 67). The South Asian community expects them to represent South Asian values and forms, and critics and audiences outside the community expect these individuals and groups to conform to their own expectations and stereotypes of what South Asians are (or should be) and what music they perform. Against these stereotypes, Dr Das of ADF observes pointedly that "my favorite Indian instrument is the bass guitar" (Sharma, 1996, p. 32), and elsewhere that "I'm playing bass guitar, Steve's playing distortion guitar, and we're more Asian than you are in what we're playing" (quoted in Hesmondhalgh and Melville, 2001, p. 97). The all-female punk band Voodoo Queens faces twice the stereotypes: being female and being South Asian. They would be marketed as a novelty act, a fad, rather than on their own merits (Huq, 1996, pp. 72–4). Sonya Aurora-Madan, lead singer of the pop group Echobelly, summarized the pressures of authenticity: "Everyone expects me to be this Asian-female-escaped-from-arranged-marriage freak" (quoted in Huq, 1996, p. 74).

These are struggles to belong to a place, to not be continually othered (named a foreigner even if third generation), stereotyped, or pigeon-holed. These are struggles not to be seen as merely derivative of non-Asian acts (Huq, 1996). For example, the Voodoo Queens were seen as Asian riot-grrrls, Fun^da^mental as the Asian Public Enemy, and so on. And these are struggles not to be relegated back to "roots" (you must be Punjabi, Bangladeshi, Pakistani). These groups are creating musical spaces to negotiate the complexity of the territory of identity. In these processes, issues of belonging and citizenship become central.

Citizenship

Citizenship in general terms has to do with a sense of belonging, invest-ment, and engagement with a particular territory. Citizenship is also a particular relationship between individuals (and groups) and a state. Citizenship is a claim to be a member of the state and to be afforded certain rights and privileges, including protection; it can be related to nationalism when the nation one is claiming as one's identity coin-cides with a particular state. At the same time citizenship is some-thing awarded and managed by the state, which dictates the policies through which one becomes a citizen and the rights and entitlements that accompany citizenship. Citizenship, therefore, can be said to have legal, political (who has a say in governing society), civic (citizenship includes the presumption that one will be active in civic affairs), and economic (who is allowed to work within the state's borders and what exceptions there are – non-citizens on worker visas) dimensions. But it also has a cultural dimension. Sunaina Maira (2004, p. 212) defines cultural citizenship as "cultural belonging in the nation, or the cultural dimensions of citizenship more broadly." Citizenship is an investment in a territory, but what if the territory is not invested in you?

May Joseph writes of being a South Asian immigrant in Tanzania in the 1970s. South Asians were brought to Tanzania by British colonial rulers (just as they had been brought to Singapore). Citizenship, Joseph argues, is something performed. One performs citizenship by territorializing according to either popular or state definitions of what it means to be a citizen: how one behaves, speaks, dresses, and acts, "the way one holds one's body, the music one consumes, or the kind of theater one produces" (Joseph, 1999, p. 4). Tanzania at the time was socialist so one of the dimensions of the performance of citizenship was the "physicality of presence . . . crowds and public displays of national affirmation" (p. 7). But there were other ways of performing Tanzanian citizenship. Joseph writes (1999, p. 2):

> I recall my own efforts at expressively staging citizenship in those early years of independence, my enthusiastic attempts to demonstrate that I was, indeed, a good Tanzanian socialist: marching along with my peers, emulating the best *ngoma* dancers by shaking my hips just so, beefing up my Swahili so that I would be among the handful of Asians accepted into the local Swahili medium secondary schools, singing Swahili songs with the right accent (Asians were constantly mocked for their poor pronunciation of Swahili), trading my skill in drawing frogs and butterflies for help from green-thumbed comrades with my *shamba*, or vegetable garden, so that I would not fail the year.

During British colonial rule, Indians had been encouraged to immigrate to Africa to work on the railroads but also to work as merchants. Eventually Indians comprised a middle class, sandwiched between the European elite and the Africans in the lower class. Eventually, nationalist movements in Tanzania, as in Uganda and elsewhere in Africa, redrew the borders of citizenship, reterritorialized along ethnic and class lines in their effort to reject colonialism. The result was the at times forcible expulsion of South Asians from those countries. Despite their best efforts and desires to belong, South Asians were deemed inauthentic citizens. What this shows is that the dimensions of citizenship discussed earlier are not uniform but can be disarticulated. Indeed, as many people become increasingly mobile in a globalized world citizenship becomes ever more complicated. Economic citizenship in many ways becomes a more salient dimension from the state's perspective. Populations deemed to have educational, economic, or labor skills needed by the state are more likely to be given the opportunity to apply for citizenship or at least claim some of the rights of citizenship. As Aihwa Ong (2006, p. 500) puts it, "entrepreneurial expatriates come to share in the rights and benefits once exclusively claimed by citizens," while some citizens in limited economic circumstances could see their entitlements and rights diminished (remember the example of Argentineans from earlier). She goes on to point out that some individuals and populations draw on universal, supra-state values and criteria, like appealing to universal human rights, to make claims on particular states for entitlements and rights. But the state ultimately has the power to reterritorialize citizenship and political shifts like those in Africa in the 1970s, or those in the US after 9/11, can make formerly welcome, productive citizens (or potential citizens) suddenly suspect based on race, ethnicity, or religion.

It is possible to use the flexibilities inherent in contemporary citizenship to one's advantage. That is, one can disarticulate citizenship from notions of nationalism or essential identity. Ong (1999, p. 6) defines *flexible citizenship* as "the cultural logics of capitalist accumulation, travel, and displacement that induce subjects to respond fluidly and opportunistically to changing political-economic conditions." For example, Ong writes about affluent Chinese immigrants who become US citizens in order to obtain a vote and also to increase their ability to shuttle between Asia and the US for business and family purposes (see Maira's, 2004, discussion). Citizenship is a strategic decision. Citizenship can be flexible, serial (depending on immigration patterns), and multiple. Los Tigres Del Norte, for example, hold dual US/Mexican citizenship, claiming at the same time the advantages of US citizenship without abdicating their Mexican cultural citizenship (see Kun, 2005).

Sunaina Maira (2004) documents a variety of citizenship strategies being mobilized in a particular community: working class and lower middle-class South Asian immigrant youth in a Cambridge, Massachusetts high school. These youth are predominantly Muslims from Gujarat in India.[5] Youth in general have a complicated relationship with citizenship, being seen as incomplete citizens, not yet mature enough to be invested with the rights of citizenship. They cannot vote and their labor is regulated by law so they cannot participate fully as citizens in these ways. Culturally, since they are not seen as full-fledged agents, still being enculturated through school and family, they are not viewed as full citizens either. However, youth do have a strong sense of citizenship, especially culturally, and are well aware of the ways they are limited by society and the state from being afforded full rights and entitlements. The group Maira is looking at "construct understandings of citizenship in relation to both the United States and one or more nations in South Asia" (Maira, 2004, p. 213). Maira discusses a number of strategies employed by the youth. We focus on two here: *flexible citizenship* and *dissenting citizenship*.

With regard to the former, as opposed to the elite Chinese discussed by Ong, Maira points out that the advantage this immigrant population seeks in its bid for US citizenship isn't just economic but that citizenship can hopefully be a "shield against the abuses of civil rights" (p. 215). That is they hope that citizenship can protect them from being taken advantage of by individuals or institutions.

> In the wake of the September 11, 2001, attacks and the subsequent war in Afghanistan, questions of citizenship and racialization have taken on new, urgent meanings for South Asian immigrant youth. Many South Asian Americans, Arab Americans, and Muslim Americans, or individuals who appeared "Muslim," have been victims of physical assaults and racial profiling. (Maira, 2005, p. 153)

The youth in Maira's study, for the most part, have lived in both South Asia and the US and still maintain strong ties with family, friends, and locales in South Asia. Though seeking US citizenship some voice the desire to return to South Asia, at least to visit, and some desire marriage with Indians from back home. Some voice an obligation to use their US citizenship to better the lives of others back home. Ong pointed out that cultural citizenship is "a dual process of self-making and being-made within webs of power linked to the nation-state and civil society" (quoted in Maira, 2004, p. 212). These youth self-make their cultural citizenship through their consumption of popular culture. For the most part they do not participate in the popular culture of the wider community of Boston and its suburbs (going to mainstream movies, concerts, and so on), but rather claim South Asian cultural citizenship through their consumption at home of South Asian popular culture. As Vijay Prashad has said more broadly of Indian Americans (called *desis*), "They live *in* America, but they are not *of* America. The desire for community draws desis to socialize with each other, to seek solace from the rigors of corporate America and to share a common vision born of this abdication from US society – to make enough money, educate their children, and then return to their respective homelands" (Prashad, 2000, p. 102). However, few ever return. For the working class youth in Maira's study, then, their sense of Asian identity is shaped by that cultural isolation, in particular by what the media represent as Asian identity. Maira shows (2004, p. 216) that for these particular youth their "identification with India or Pakistan is based largely on Bollywood (Hindi) films, Indian television serials, and Indian music they access through video, satellite TV, and the Internet." For the youth in Maira's study, while they seek cultural citizenship transnationally and hope for legal citizenship in the US, they are laboring locally (economic citizenship) in low-wage shift-work in fast food, retail, convenience stores, and restaurants which gives them little time to socialize. They work hard but are denied the entry points (for example, social networks, contacts, and know-how) that will lead them to economic advancement. They are in a position to see through the neoliberal promise that citizenship and hard work will lead to success, recognizing what their limitations are and what resources are denied them.

This particular perspective gives rise to a second strategy of citizenship which Maira notes: *dissenting citizenship*. Post-9/11 Muslims have been popularly equated with terrorists and considered "noncitizens"; they are marked in popular discourse as undeniably and essentially foreign (and potentially dangerous). Within these historical conditions Maira (2004, p. 222) sees some of the youth engaged in a dissenting citizenship: "a citizenship based on a critique and affirmation of human rights that means one has to stand apart at some moments, even as one stands together with others who are often faceless, outside the borders of the nation." These students affirm rather than bury their Muslim identity and contest the equation of Muslims and terrorists. In some ways, as youth and students these individuals are more protected (or at least given more leeway, an allowance or tolerance for their youth), better able to speak out than their parents whose livelihood (and even continued stay in the US) is more precariously based on public opinion. However, these opinions are just as liable to be dismissed and not considered seriously because of the youth of their advocates. Despite this, the students are able to speak to connections between the treatment of immigrants in the US and US foreign policy (especially the wars in Afghanistan and Iraq). They exhibit what Maira, following Paul Clarke (1996), calls a *deep citizenship*, to see themselves and those on the receiving end of US foreign policy as common world citizens. Deep citizenship is "an ethics of care that is fundamentally about a moral and political engagement with the world that extends beyond the state" (Maira, 2004, p. 222). In this claim of belonging, a territorialization based on an ethic of care for the other grounded in their everyday lives as transnationals, the students find a ground for civic engagement and participation in a state to which they wish to belong.

Desis in America

Maira has studied other populations of South Asian immigrants and second- and third-generation youth and delineates a number of factors they contend with in their everyday territorializations (2002). The first factor is their parents' financial expectations. Second-generation youth who came of age in the 1980s and 1990s tended to be children of a wave of Indian professionals who immigrated to the US after 1965. These professionals soon established themselves in the middle and upper middle class and emphasized to their children the American dream of upward mobility, often dictating particular appropriate career paths for their children (for example, doctors). However, the second factor is that changing social and economic circumstances generally in the US mean that the opportunities available to the parents are not necessarily available to their children, who may have to struggle to meet their parents' standards of living. So parental pressure for success and the anxiety of trying to meet those expectations are two of the factors in how these youth structure their sense of identity and the spaces of their everyday life. A third factor is the racism pervasive in American society at large, particularly dominant racist notions of who South Asians are and what they are like, accompanied by racist slurs and violence against South Asians. At the same time the fourth factor is the concurrent notion of Indians as a "model minority," successful and not causing social unrest or draining social resources. This notion has been challenged by subsequent waves of working class South Asian immigrants who were not as economically advantaged as the earlier wave and therefore less successful. But across the board immigrants have to deal with the fifth factor, the catch-22 of immigrants negotiating the landscape of citizenship in the US. Maira (2002, p. 189) terms this the "tension between assimilationist and pluralist models of national identity in the United States." On the one hand one is expected to blend in to the melting pot (become "American"), but on the other hand one is expected to maintain a root identity (remaining forever "Indian-American").

Maira is studying college students, and so the sixth factor in youth territorialization is the particular culture of the US college campus, in particular two aspects. The first of these is that students may find themselves in a community with a larger number of desi youth like themselves (desi is a self-nominated designation for people of South Asian descent), and that such ethnic groups tend to set up exclusive cliques (Filipinos over there, Chinese over here). The second aspect of the college experience is its emphasis on multiculturalism. Courses dealing with race, ethnicity, and identity enlighten youth to the construction of identity. This in turn leads to a self-conscious exploration of one's own identity which tends to mean a search for roots and cultural authenticity (Prashad (2000, pp. 190–1) calls this " 'reverse assimilation,' the rediscovery of one's ethnicity and the urge to engage that difference in one's social life"). This search reinforces the trend of collecting in ethnic-derived groups who together explore, construct, and strengthen particular notions of ethnic identity. In particular, this sense of collective "Indianness" can include developing or emphasizing an Indian accent, speaking a South Asian language, attending religious and cultural festivals (even if one never did so growing up), and hanging out with other South Asians consuming South Asian cultural products like music or film. The availability of these cultural resources is the seventh factor in youth territorialization.

The construction of this Indian identity incorporates very particular elements, meaning that this is a selective identity. Particular music is drawn on, either traditional classical music or new bhangra hybrids (more on this in a moment); particular films are viewed (especially Hindi films). This version of India, and consequently what is considered Indian when one is judging oneself and one's peers for cultural inclusivity (that is, when territorializing a community of authentic desis), is determined in part by the media. TV shows and films are taken to be more representative than they are of the Indian population, and so the assumed look and lifestyle of the authentic Indian back home tends to be more wealthy, more ethnically from Northern India (more pale), more religiously conservative (and Hindu). In short, Indian film stars, who tend to be much thinner, whiter, and more western looking than the general Indian population, are taken to be typical Indians by desi youth (Maira, p. 171). In addition these youth emphasize the cultural dimensions of India when constructing notions of authenticity. As Maira (2002, p. 15) asks, "Why are possession of Indian language skills, socialization with other Indian Americans, and interest in Indian films considered *more* Indian than engagement with social and political issues relevant to contemporary India and to Indians in the diaspora?" Partly this has to do with the negotiated citizenship desis as a model minority inhabit: acceptance for their economic capital but at the price of their political activism. As Vijay Prashad (2000, pp. 101–2) puts it, "In the United States the bulk of the desi community seems to have moved away from active political struggles . . . The bargain revolves around the sale of the desi political soul in exchange for the license to accumulate economic wealth through hard work and guile." Partly, this is because this version of Indianness is colored by nostalgia which talk of social change and politics disturbs. Nostalgia is a key component of these desi territorializations, constructed out of their parents' selective memories of how India used to be (not acknowledging changes since), their own desire for India to be a certain way (a touchstone of authenticity and tradition, almost premodern) which emphasizes elements of spirituality and history. This nostalgic view comports well with Western Orientalist stereotypes of India and Indians reflected in films such as *Gandhi, Passage to India, City of God*, and so on (see Mitra, 1999). It is little surprising, given this nostalgic view of India, that there tends to be great financial support for more conservative religious and political movements in India through conservative cultural organizations in the US – cultural organizations to which desis turn searching for their authentic culture (Prashad, 2000).

   This Indian identity is but one part of a desi's daily life, lived, in the case of Maira's study, in New York City. Drawing on all these factors and contexts, second generation middle class Indian youth have created their own cultural spaces, similar to the soundsystem and day-timer cultures discussed previously. They have fused bhangra-remix culture (incorporating the new British bhangra and Hindi film music) with New York club culture to create their own exclusively South Asian spaces for cultural creation and reinvention, a space where the youthful desi community can be created, reinforced, and policed. These are spaces where Indian authenticity is performed, but not as a staid mimicry of tradition and classical performance, but as a remix of a number of cultural elements. Though considered fiercely South Asian, these spaces draw on the British bhangra and new Asian music scene; the circulation of select South Asian films, TV shows, and popular music; and the white and black popular culture scenes in the US, particularly hip hop and club culture. They can wear hip hop fashion or clubwear and perform Indian dance moves most likely learned from Indian films. This is the *cool*, the last element in desi territorialization, the hip party scene. The cool is not in opposition to nostalgia, but infused with it. Though this scene is marked by hybrid styles (in terms of music and dress) this is still considered a site of Indian cultural authenticity. This is strategic antiessentialism, using the antiessentialist practice of borrowing from other cultures to strategically "return to the notion of an exclusive ethnic community and redraw the boundaries of insidership" (Maira, 2002, p. 80). As mentioned above, these are spaces where authenticity is performed, where cultural belonging is read off from one's style and performance. If one doesn't participate, one is a "fake Indian." And if one does participate, how one does so indicates one's level of authenticity. This club culture is a site of surveillance of cultural authenticity (one imposed by the desi youth themselves, not by their parents). This surveillance weighs more heavily on the young women, presumed bearers of cultural authenticity, who are scrutinized more than men. What a woman wears reflects on her Indianness. There is a tension between dressing like a "girlfriend" (in sexy, Western clubwear) and dressing like a "future wife." Both are considered culturally Indian, part of this new cultural territory, but the latter will be judged as more Indian. The club is the space where these things can be negotiated, where one can play with how one wants to be perceived, where one can escape one's daily identity, or use the space to reaffirm it.

The factors outlined by Maira can play out in a number of ways. They are not, in the last instance, determinative. That is, they do not produce uniform subjects but are a set of conditions to be negotiated (and a set of conditions not unique to desis). Such negotiation is exemplified in a number of recent films, mostly comedies, that deal with the Indian-American experience: *ABCD* (1999), *American Chai* (2001), *American Desi* (2001), *Ball and Chain* (2004), and *Dude, Where's the Party* (originally, *Where's the Party Yaar?* 2003). I want to briefly talk about two of these, *ABCD* and *American Desi*, not because they are necessarily representative (and I'm also not making claims as to the quality or relative merits of either film), but illustrative of the issues of territorialization.

The first film is Piyush Dinker Pandya's (2001) *American Desi*. The film opens in the stereotypical suburban bedroom of a teenage American boy. The boy in question is packing for college. The first shot of the film is of an American flag hanging on the wall, with sports trophies set out in front of it. Posters of rock stars and pin-ups (like Jenny McCarthy) hang on the wall as well, and we see pictures of baseball teams, a certificate from the New Jersey Boys State, and a picture of a blonde prom date. We see the youth playing a drum kit, wearing a backwards baseball cap. We are meant to read this territory as a middle class white cultural space. It is not until he turns around that we realize that he is of Indian descent. This is Krisna, who prefers the more Anglo "Kris," who is heading off to college with his best (white) buddy, Eric. Kris is profoundly embarrassed by his parents ritual blessing as they depart (barely tolerated with a lot of eye-rolling). Kris and Eric drive off, exchanging jock/frat boy banter about how exciting college is going to be. Kris embodies a complete rejection of Indian culture. The purpose of the film is to recuperate Kris back to his Indian roots. It cannot allow him to be "American" and insists that he embrace being "Indian-American" (with emphasis on the former). The film, then, can be seen as a reterritorialization, the policing of citizenship. The emphasis on cultural and ethnic roots (in this and many, many other films) designates particular populations as Other, as always and forever hyphenated-Americans.

Kris arrives at college and discovers to his dismay that he has been assigned to a dorm suite filled with a diverse range of Indian stereotypes: the Sikh with a turban, the devout Muslim, the desi who tries to be Black (awkwardly performing hip hop moves and slang). The more Kris tries to distance himself from his suitemates, and hang out with Eric and his white friends, the more he seems to be pulled in to the campus desi community. Kris then falls for Nina, a desi who seems to have managed to balance the Indian and the American cultural contexts, but who has a deep love of Indian culture. To woo her, Kris realizes that he needs to be Indian and not American. His chief rival for Nina's affections is well versed in Indian culture and does his best to out Kris as a fake Indian. The rest of the film presents Kris's journey of learning how to be Indian: from disastrous attempts at learning how to cook Indian food, watching Indian films, and learning traditional dances, to helping to organize an Indian cultural festival on campus. In the process he has to deal with his American cultural reactions to Indian culture, for example his loud retorts of frustration while watching Bollywood films: the 3+ hour length, the multiple elaborate dance numbers, the illogical plots. In a way, Kris's journey parallels that of the Indian-American college youth of Maira's study: confronted by a large desi population and territorialized by both the desi community and broader community as Indian, and exploring and accepting a particular version of cultural roots. Though the films asks us to identify with Kris and accept his transformation, it also positions the viewer as being outside Indian culture. The stereotypes of Indians represented are broad and played for laughs, poking fun at their inept attempts to appear cool or simply their obliviousness to American culture (for example the utter cluelessness of an Indian graduate student who instructs a class while his fly hangs open). In the end it seems as if Kris has little choice in his journey, and therefore in his identity.

An earlier film, Krutin Patel's (1999) *ABCD* offers a bit more nuanced view of a similar dilemma. ABCD refers to the phrase, "American Born Confused Desi" used to identify the cultural crisis of second generation desi youth. The film is about Anju, an Indian widow living in New Jersey to be close to her two children (born in India but raised in the US). Anju remains culturally traditional, with expectations that her children will succeed in business, retain their cultural heritage, and marry Indians. The cultural territory of her house is Indian; her son remarks at one point that it doesn't feel like New Jersey, as they sit on the swing on her back porch. Her son, Raj, an accountant, tries his best to please his mother and has been engaged for two years to Tejal in an arranged affair. But he is obviously dragging his feet in embracing fully his cultural heritage (that is, going through with the wedding), and a series of events lead him to a crisis of cultural identity. First, he is passed over for a promotion because he doesn't have the extroverted gregariousness of his white co-worker (and best friend), though he is clearly the harder worker and the better accountant (this work ethic and submissiveness to authority is assumed in the film to be the result of his culture). Second, he falls for the white woman who takes his friend's old position. Anju's daughter, Nina, is much like Kris in *American Desi*: she considers Indian culture embarrassing, doesn't dress Indian (even when attending a traditional Indian wedding), professes ignorance of any cultural traditions, and dates only white men (apparently sleeping with as many as she can, in stark contrast to traditional expectations for Indian women). Her crisis of identity comes when Ashok, a childhood friend, arrives from India. Ashok and Nina are set up by Anju, and they go out on a date. She discovers feelings for him, but at the same time a white man she used to be engaged to comes back into her life. A film about identity crisis and search for self, *ABCD* does not present its characters with a predetermined path – there is no clear destiny for either Raj or Nina and their decisions are not necessarily the "correct" ones.

Of course, not every second generation desi undergoes identity crisis, and it would be profoundly unfair to suggest that they do. As Rupa Huq (1996, pp. 65–6) has written, these sorts of assumptions reinforce "dominant representations of Asians – caught between two cultures, desultory, directionless, confused. It is, however, rather reductive to see Asian youth as perpetual victims of the system when the reality of dual or indeed multiple identities is much more complex." The processes of cultural territorialization are not just about crises and transformation, but the everyday construction of identity. This chapter has presented a variety of examples of these processes, from Faye Wong's strategic border crossing to Dick Lee's strategic pan-Asian identity to Apache Indian's syncretic, rhizomic audioscape, we've seen how cultural identity is constructed, contested, and invested. These examples are certainly not exhaustive, and they are not meant to be, but hopefully they are suggestive.

Notes

1   In another example of how quickly one's inclusion in the broader com-
    munity (one's cultural citizenship) can shift, consider the case of South
    Asians and Arab Americans post 9/11. Though these groups have histor-
    ically held shifting positions of inclusion and exclusion throughout the
    twentieth century, by the 1990s many of the wealthier members of these
    groups had achieved "model minority" status, becoming for most intents
    and purposes "white." What Louise Cainkar and Sunaina Maira have called
    the post-9/11 backlash found many in these groups stripped of legal
    citizenship and residency, and most stripped of cultural citizenship;
    profiled as terrorists, criminals, and dangerous outsiders, they became
    criminalized, subject to increase surveillance and categorical suspicion.

> There are important alliances that need to be forged between these and
> other communities that would go beyond the confines of multiculturalist
> "difference" and build connections based on an analysis of political and
> material processes. For example, South Asian, Arab, and Muslim Americans
> who now have heightened concerns about issues of detention have much
> to learn from African Americans, Latinos, and Native Americans who have
> long fought against racism – especially that of the prison-industrial com-
> plex, and advocated for the rights of political prisoners (Cainkar and Maira,
> 2005, p. 20).

2   Tracing the cultural form of the sound system even further back, Dick
    Hebdige locates reggae's roots in black American music after World
    War II (1987; cited in Rose 1994). Sound systems were developed by
    Jamaicans as a way to play imported American R&B to a large crowd.
    Jamaican sound system culture imported back to New York with Jamaican
    immigrants became an influential source for the creation of rap music
    (Rose, 1994).

3   As Marie Gillespie (1995, pp. 45–6) writes of bhangra, "[i]t has become
    a focal point for the public emergence of a British Asian youth culture
    which transcends traditional divisions and aspires to a sense of ethnic
    unity."

4   See, for example, John Hutnyk's (2004) discussion of pop group Kula
    Shaker's appropriations of Indian exoticisms to further their music.

5   Maira (2005, p. 154) points out that the school itself is very diverse, "with
    students from Latin America, the Caribbean, Africa, and Asia. Students
    from India, Pakistan, Bangladesh, and Afghanistan constitute the largest
    Muslim population in the school, followed by youth from Ethiopia,
    Somalia, and Morocco."

Conclusion:
Opening Windows

At the end of Chapter 5, I stated that the processes of cultural territorialization were not just about crises and transformation, but about the everyday construction of identity. In this process, identity should be conjunctive, an *and*. However, broader cultural and social structures force identity to be disjunctive, to be an *or*. Choice should not be about false dichotomies, one or the other. The process of discovering roots and routes could be productive and rhizomic, producing new identities that incorporate and draw from multiple cultural territories. But the discovery of roots can also be a containment strategy – one is now *that* and not *this*. How, then, to be an And in a world of Ors?

I had not started out to write a book about identity, but rather one on culture and territory; to look at cultural processes as spatial, territorial. I liked the idea (and the image) of culture as a series of trajectories across spaces – vectors of objects, stories, meanings, ideas that we try to marshal, but which also catch us up and sweep us away. But identity is always a product, presumption, and strata of these processes. My goal, then, was to start talking about these processes, or at least make the point that there *are* these sorts of processes. What these processes look like, the factors involved, the possibilities for agency, and so on, will vary dramatically. Therefore, I hope I have been clear (though perhaps overly repetitive and pedantic) in stating that the examples given here are suggestive and generative, and not representative or exhaustive. I'm not interested (in this particular project) in arguing for a limited set of processes and influences – for example, that culture is always a struggle against tradition, parents, teachers, priests, corporations, and so on. The particular configuration of processes varies by culture, history, class, gender, sexuality, ethnicity, and so on.

But what do we learn from these examples and conceptual discussions? What, in the end, should we do in a globalized world? How should we live? One theme to consider in responding to this question is to think of the skill sets necessary to make one's way in this world. We need to pay attention to the experience of various peoples, from the global elite of business and tourist class who crisscross the globe, to third culture kids and global nomads, to diasporic and immigrant populations. George Lipsitz, for example, argues that we need to pay close attention to the experience of immigrants and the urban poor:

> The populations best prepared for cultural conflict and political contestation in a globalized world economy may well be the diasporic communities of displaced Africans, Asians, and Latin Americans created by the machinations of world capitalism over the centuries. These populations, long accustomed to code switching, syncretism, and hybridity may prove far more important for what they *possess* in cultural terms than for what they appear to *lack* in the political lexicon of the nation state. (Lipsitz, 1994, pp. 30–1, emphasis in original)

At the same time, we need to recognize that mobility, immigration, and so on do not necessarily bring these skills or even give one a political or ethical outlook. That is, being diasporic in and of itself doesn't necessarily give one appropriate agency or insight into global processes (Ong, 1999), though it potentially provides important perspective and a set of cultural tools and skills (code switching, syncretism, hybridity). We just need to be careful to not fetishize mobility.

A second theme to consider when pondering the question is the politics of youth culture. A focus on global youth lends urgency to questions of globalization because issues of culture seem most acute when they concern youth. A crisis of youth is a crisis of cultural continuation and contestation. A focus on youth also raises issues of cultural creativity, cultural imperialism, economic hardship, and political and cultural citizenship. But in the end, as I stated in Chapter 3, the issues of global youth are issues all ages face. Cindi Katz's new politics of youth is really a new politics for us all.

Third, we need to consider what the perspective of cultural territorialization brings to these issues (issues that have been hashed over in any number of other disciplines, forums, and publications). For me, what it brings is an emphasis on the fluidity, flexibility, and permeability of identity. Cultural territorialization of whatever scale (region, nation, group, individual) is always permeable, formed in relation to and flow with elsewheres and elsewhens, though the borders at times become hardened by habit, fear, and weaponry. Theorizing and presenting these case studies as I have is to view them through an ethics of territorialization, one summed up in a perhaps too-oft-quoted passage by Mahatma Gandhi (1921, p. 170):

> I do not want my house to be walled in on all sides and my windows to be stuffed. I want the cultures of all the lands to be blown about my house as freely as possible. But I refuse to be blown off my feet by any.

The image Gandhi presents is one that stays with me as I think about processes of home-making: culture is the wind and the wall.

What I'm advocating, then, is a *cosmopolitanism* of a sort. But let me specify a bit what I mean by that term since it's yet another term (like global youth or world music) that has problematic connotations. Two key connotations I want to distance myself from are the connotation of cosmopolitan as urban elite and the connotation of cosmopolitan as being focused solely on the global, on the world as a whole and ignoring and disparaging any focus on the local. Ulf Hannerz (1996, pp. 102, 103) writes that cosmopolitanism is a "mode of managing meaning," and that "a more genuine cosmopolitanism is first of all an orientation, a willingness to engage with the Other. It entails an intellectual and esthetic openness toward divergent cultural experiences, a search for contrasts rather than uniformity." That openness to the Other, the winds sweeping through your window, is one element of cosmopolitanism. And this cosmopolitanism is not the reserve of the elites. As philosopher Kwame Anthony Appiah (2006, p. xviii) writes, "[t]he well-traveled polyglot is as likely to be among the worst off as among the best off – as likely to be found in a shantytown as at the Sorbonne." Recall the code-switching syn-cretism of musicians and youth discussed in this book, and the slum dwellers Lipsitz pointed to above. Indeed, the elites tend to travel within a comfortable territorialization guaranteed not to disturb them. Hannerz (1996, p. 107) points out that "the institutions of the trans-national cultures tend to be organized so as to make people from western Europe and North America feel as much at home as pos-sible (by using their languages, for one thing)." This is not real cos-mopolitanism. To grasp and affirm the notion of cosmopolitanism as orientation towards the Other does not deny one's connections to family, friends, community, culture, or nation. It is not to deny all these processes of identity. But it does mean that we shouldn't fetishize these to the detriment of all else, elevating these above all else. Pride and a sense of belonging to family, community, culture, and nation are important, but I always worry when they become all important. Excessive flag waving always makes me nervous. Note, I'm not saying that *all* flag waving makes me nervous, just excessive flag waving, when it drowns everything else out, narrows our vision, so that we close ourselves to Others. I'll give you an example. A few years ago, the film *Million Dollar Baby* was generating quite a bit of controversy. At issue in public discussions of the film was a ques-tion of euthanasia and right to life. But much more disturbing and controversial for me when I watched the film were the scenes earlier on where white Irish crowds at boxing matches begin to chant in unison (and in Gaelic) "my blood, my blood" in support of a white Irish-American boxer played by Hilary Swank as she pummeled dark skinned opponents in the ring, scenes which seemed to pass without comment in the press. It's those levels of fervent nationalism and prim-ordialism, especially when accepted without comment or resistance, that always make me reach for my passport. As Appiah (2006, p. xvi) has put it, "the one thought that cosmopolitans share is that no local loyalty can ever justify forgetting that each human being has respons-ibilities to every other."

Openness to Others is one aspect of cosmopolitanism; the other element is care for the other. This is something different than simply being open to new experiences and people, but of feeling a concern, an obligation, and a care for them. In a way, this is Maira's deep citizen-ship discussed in Chapter 5. But why should we care for strangers?

Why should we care for others whom we will never meet? Let me approach this question by looking at a specific corollary: why should I care about all these examples in this book? Why should I care about how others live and cope? After all, our lives tend to be busy enough with all our local concerns and activities (job, family, friends, community) to worry about someone else on the other side of the world. To this I have two answers.

The first answer, the more pedagogical answer, is that engaging with these stories makes us personally reflective, considering our own place in the world and how globalization affects each of us. That is, one hopes they provoke thought on the part of the reader to self-reflect, to see one's everyday life in a slightly different way, to realize the ways the global is always already a quite real part of one's everyday life and that global processes are a part of who we are and what we do – even if one is not traveling, moving, grooving to the beat of a foreign drummer. And if that thought and reflection are provoked, so much the better. However, hopefully this reflection is more along the lines of tracing vectors and flows and noting practices of territorialization and deterritorialization rather than simply seeking one's identity. As Paul Gilroy writes, the focus on individual identity – marked by the question, "who am I?" – turns one away from the problems of the world. Asking that question:

> is a problematic gesture that all too often culminates in the substitution of an implosive and therefore anti-social form of self-scrutiny for the discomfort and the promise of public political work which does not assume either solidarity or community but works instead to bring them into being and then to make them democratic. (Gilroy, 2006, p. 383)

So, if the only result of pondering these issues is an individual navelgazing, then we're missing an important element of cosmopolitanism. If we conclude that globalization only matters when it affects me, then we've fallen prey to the neoliberal ideology that places all social, economic, cultural, and political agency on the shoulders of the individual. To see people only as individuals reduces them, I would argue. We are the products of our spaces and our interactions with others. We are always already more than ourselves as individuals. The cosmopolitan would say that globalization matters even if I'm not the one losing his or her job. At the same time it's good not to abstract out the experience or plight of others, to speak of globalization in a too-general sense, disconnected from the lives of those affected. I considered giving this conclusion the title, *Forget Globalization*. Besides being provocative, the title would be a reminder that a focus on globalization as a general process distracts us from the plights of individuals and groups living these processes. When reading stories of globalization, not just here but wherever we encounter them in our daily lives, asking the old questions that Ariel Dorfman and Armand Mattelart wielded so nicely gets us started to think about the broader implications of what we're being told: who benefits if we see the world this way? And, who is missing from this view of the world? To consider that there are those who do not benefit from this view of the world or are absent from its pretty, narrow pictures is to begin to recognize the Other, open oneself to the Other, and perhaps, maybe, even care.

A second answer to why we should care to listen to stories of how others live and cope is one I borrow from Appiah, (2006, p. 78) who is arguing for this same kind of cosmopolitanism I am discussing here. He writes: "I am urging that we should learn about people in other places, take an interest in their civilizations, their arguments, their errors, their achievements, not because that will bring us to agreement, but because it will help us get used to one another."

Getting used to one another. Entering into a dialogue with one another. This doesn't presume that we will all agree in the end, indeed Appiah doubts that we will, but that we can learn from one another. Cosmopolitanism, in this way, is not a solution to the dilemmas raised in this book, but another way of framing them. It is, as Appiah puts it, a *challenge*. So my second answer as to why we should care about stories of globalization, of punk groups in Bali, hip hop in Korea, second generation Indians in New York, is that they get us used to one another, and, eventually, used to living in a bigger world. Knowledge alone is not the answer, and is no guarantee of an ethical response to the world – indeed, Appiah argues that we must reject the argument that "prejudice derives only from ignorance, that intimacy must breed amity" (2006, p. 8). The Orientalists, after all, were quite knowledgeable about their subject matter. Rather, the process of engaging others, their stories, and stories of them, and of getting used to them, "is one of the central human ways of learning to align our responses to the world" (p. 29), and in so doing, "it will help us decide . . . how we should act in the world" (p. 30). And if we take this idea of cosmopolitanism, or deep citizenship, seriously, then we must realize that there are no Others, only others, finding their way through their ordinary everyday lives.

References

Ahmad, Ali Nobil (2001). Whose Underground? Asian Cool and the Poverty of Hybridity. *Third Text*, Spring, 71–84.

Ahmed, Sara (1999). Home and Away: Narratives of Migration and Estrangement. *International Journal of Cultural Studies*, 2(3), 329–47.

Almada, Natalia (producer) (2006). Al otro lado [documentary]. *POV*. Broadcast on PBS, August 1, 2006.

Anderson, Benedict (1983). *Imagined Communities: Reflections on the Origin and Spread of Nationalism*. New York: Verso.

Ang, Ien, and Stratton, Jon (1997). The Singapore Way of Multiculturalism: Western Concepts/Asian Cultures. *New Formations*, 31, 51–66.

Appadurai, Arjun (1996). *Modernity at Large: Cultural Dimensions of Globalization*. Minneapolis: University of Minnesota Press.

Appiah, Kwame Anthony (2006). *Cosmopolitanism: Ethics in a World of Strangers*. New York: Norton.

Back, Les (1995). X Amount of sat siri akal! Apache Indian, Reggae Music and the Cultural Intermezzo. *New Formations*, 27(2), 128–47.

Back, Les (1996). *New Ethnicities and Urban Culture: Racisms and Multiculture in Young Lives*. London: UCL Press.

Barber, Benjamin (1996). *Jihad v. McWorld: How Globalism and Tribalism are Reshaping the World*. New York: Ballantine Books.

Barrett, James (1996). World Music, Nation, and Post-Colonialism. *Cultural Studies*, 10(2), 237–47.

Baulch, Emma (2002). Creating a Scene: Balinese Punk's Beginnings. *International Journal of Cultural Studies*, 5(2), 153–77.

Beech, Hannah (n.d.). School Daze. *TimeAsia.Com*. Accessed from http://www.time.com/time/asia/features/asian_education/cover.html on 6/15/06.

References

Bennett, Andy (2001). *Cultures of Popular Music*. Maidenhead, UK: Open University Press.

Bourdieu, Pierre (1990). *In Other Words: Essays Towards a Reflexive Sociology*. Trans. Matthew Adamson. Stanford, CA: Stanford University Press.

Boym, Svetlana (1994). *Common Places: Mythologies of Everyday Life in Russia*. Cambridge, MA: Harvard University Press.

Brennan, Timothy (2003). Global Youth and Local Pleasure: Cuba and the Right to Popular Music. In Daniel Fischlin and Ajay Heble (eds.), *Rebel Musics: Human Rights, Resistant Sounds, and the Politics of Music Making* (pp. 210–31). New York: Black Rose Books.

Brown, Mark, and Torres, Luc (2006). G-had and Suicide Bombers: The Rapper who Likens Bin Laden to Che Guevara. *The Guardian Online*, 28 June, Accessed from http://arts.guardian.co.uk/print/0,,329515676-110427,00.html on 8/15/2006.

Burrell, Ian (2003, 17 October). Invisible Superstars. *The Independent Arts and Books Review*, 2–4.

Cainkar, Louise and Maira, Sunaina Marr (2005). Targeting Arab/Muslim/South Asian Americans: Criminalization and Cultural Citizenship. *Amerasia Journal*, 31(3), 1–27.

Chambers, Iain (1990). *Border Dialogues*. New York: Routledge.

Chan, Ka Yan (n.d.). *Exploring Youth Subculture in Hong Kong: A Case Study on the Local Band LazyMuthaFucka (LMF)*, MPhil Thesis, Chinese University of Hong Kong.

Cho, Han Haejoang (n.d.) Youth, Internet and Culture: The Haja Experimental Project. Unpublished Paper.

Chu, Yiu Wai (2006). The Transformation of Local Identity in Hong Kong Cantopop Lyrics (1970s–1990s). *Perfect Beat*, 7(4), 32–51.

Clarke, Paul Barry (1996). *Deep Citizenship*. Chicago: Pluto Press.

Dávila, Arlene (2001). *Latinos, Inc.: The Marketing and Making of a People*. Berkeley: University of California Press.

Dávila, Arlene (2002). Talking Back: Spanish Media and US Latinidad. In Michelle Habell-Pallán and Mary Romero (eds.), *Latino/a Popular Culture* (pp. 25–37). New York: New York University Press.

Davis, Susan (1996). The Theme Park: Global Industry and Cultural Form. *Media, Culture and Society*, 18, 399–422.

De Certeau, Michel (1984). *The Practice of Everyday Life*. Trans. Steve Rendall. Berkeley: University of California Press.

Deleuze, Gilles, and Guattari, Félix (1987). *A Thousand Plateaus: Capitalism and Schizophrenia*. Trans. Brian Massumi. Minneapolis: University of Minnesota Press.

References

Dorfman, Ariel, and Mattelart, Armand (1991). *How To Read Donald Duck: Imperialist Ideology in the Disney Comic*. Trans. David Kunzle. New York: International General.

Dorland, Michael (ed.) (1996). *The Cultural Industries in Canada: Problems, Policies and Prospects*. Toronto: Lorimer.

Dudrah, Rajinder K. (2002). Drum'n'dhol: British Bhangra Music and Diasporic South Asian Identity Formation. *European Journal of Cultural Studies*, 5(3), 363–83.

Dwyer, Claire (1998). Contested Identities: Challenging Dominant Representations of Young British Muslim Women. In Tracey Skelton and Gill Valentine (eds.), *Cool Places: Geographies of Youth Culture* (pp. 50–65). New York: Routledge.

Ellwood, Wayne (2001). *The No-Nonsense Guide to Globalization*. London: Verso.

Ender, Morten G. (2002). *Military Brats and Other Global Nomads: Growing Up in Organization Families*. Westport, CT: Praeger.

Epstein, Stephen J. (2000). Anarchy in the UK, Solidarity in the ROK: Punk Rock Comes to Korea. *Acta Koreana*, 3, 1–34. Accessed from http://www2.gol.com/users/coynerhm/punk_rock_comes_to_korea.htm on 10/27/2004.

Epstein, Stephen J. (2001). Nationalism and Globalization in Korean Underground Music: Our Nation, Volume One. In Roy Starrs (ed.), *Asian Nationalism in an Age of Globalization* (pp. 374–87). Richmond, Surrey: Japan Library.

Epstein, Stephen J. (n.d.). Never Mind the Bollocks, Here's Choson Punk. *IIAS Newsletter Online*, 26. Accessed from http://www.iias.nl/iiasn/26/theme/26T5.html on 7/30/2006.

Epstein, Stephen and Tangherlini, Timothy (producers) (2001). *Our Nation: A Korean Punk Rock Community* [film]. New York: Filmakers Library.

Erni, John (2001). Like a Postcolonial Culture: Hong Kong Re-Imagined. *Cultural Studies*, 15(3/4), 389–418.

Featherstone, Mike (ed.) (1990). *Global culture: Nationalism, Globalization, and Modernity*. Newbury Park, CA: Sage.

Feld, Steve (1994). Notes on "World Beat." In Charles Keil and Steve Feld (eds.), *Music Grooves: Essays and Dialogues* (pp. 238–46). Chicago: University of Chicago Press.

Feld, Steve (2000). A Sweet Lullaby for World Music. *Public Culture*, 12(1), 145–71.

Fiske, John (1989). *Understanding Popular Culture*. Winchester, MA: Unwin Hyman.

References

Flores, Juan (1994). Puerto Rican and Proud, Boyee! Rap, Roots and Amnesia. In Andrew Ross and Tricia Rose (eds.), *Microphone Fiends: Youth Music and Youth Culture* (pp. 89–98). New York: Routledge.

Flores, Juan (2000). *From Bomba to Hip-Hop: Puerto Rican Culture and Latino Identity*. New York: Columbia University Press.

Forman, Murray (2002). *The 'Hood Comes First: Race, Space, and Place in Rap and Hip-Hop*. Middletown, CT: Wesleyan University Press.

Fung, Anthony (forthcoming). Fandom, Feminism, and Faye Wong: The Oriental Madonna in Question. Unpublished manuscript.

Fung, Anthony, and Curtin, Michael (2002). The Anomalies of being Faye (Wong): Gender Politics in Chinese Popular Music. *International Journal of Cultural Studies*, 5(3), 263–90.

Gandhi, Mohandas Karamchand "Mahatma" (1921). *The Collected Works of Mahatma Gandhi*, New Delhi 1958–84, Vol. 6, June 1, 1921, p. 170.

Garofalo, Reebee (1992). Introduction. In Reebee Garofalo (ed.), *Rockin' the Boat: Mass Music and Mass Movements* (pp. 1–13). Boston: South End Press.

Generation Y earns $211 billion a year and spends $172 billion annually (2003). *Harris Interactive*. Accessed from www.harrisinteractive.com on 9/9/2003.

Gillespie, Marie (1995). *Television, Ethnicity, and Cultural Change*. New York: Routledge.

Gilroy, Paul (1992). It's a Family Affair. In G. Dent (ed.), *Black Popular Culture*. Seattle: Bay Press.

Gilroy, Paul (1993). *The Black Atlantic: Modernity and Double Consciousness*. New York: Verso.

Gilroy, Paul (2006). British Cultural Studies and the Pitfalls of Identity. In Meenakshi Gigi and Douglas M. Kellner (eds.), *Media and Cultural Studies: KeyWorks* (Revised edn.) (pp. 381–95). Malden, MA: Blackwell.

Gómez-Peña, Guillermo (1991). *Border Brujo* [videorecording]. Isaac Artenstein (Producer). New York: Third World Newsreel.

Goodwin, Andrew, and Gore, Joe (1995). World Beat and the Cultural Imperialism Debate. In Ron Sakolsky and Fred Wei-han Ho (eds.), *Sounding Off! Music as Subversion/Resistance/Revolution* (pp. 121–31). New York: Autonomedia.

Grossberg, Lawrence, Wartella, Ellen, Whitney, D. Charles, and Wise, J. Macgregor (2006). *MediaMaking* (2nd edn.). Thousand Oaks, CA: Sage.

Hall, Stuart (1981). The Whites of Their Eyes: Racist Ideologies and the Media. In George Bridges and Rosalind Brunt (eds.), *Silver Linings: Some Strategies for the Eighties* (pp. 28–52). London: Lawrence and Wishart.

Hall, Stuart (1995). New Cultures for Old. In Doreen Massey and Pat Jess (eds.), *A Place in the World? Places, Cultures and Globalization* (pp. 175–213). Basingstoke, UK: Open University Press.

Hall, Stuart, and Jefferson, Tony (eds.) (1976). *Resistance Through Rituals: Youth Subcultures in Post-War Britain*. Boston: Unwin Hyman.

Hannerz, Ulf (1996). *Transnational Connections: Culture, People, Places*. New York: Routledge.

Hau, Louis (2001, 25 August). Drug Records Helps Punk Thrive in South Korea. *Billboard*, 51. Accessed via EBSCO Host, 7/30/2006.

Hebdige, Dick (1979). *Subculture: The Meaning of Style*. New York: Methuen.

Hebdige, Dick (1987). *Cut'n'Mix: Culture, Identity, and Caribbean Music*. New York: Routledge.

Hebdige, Dick (1988). *Hiding in the Light: On Images and Things*. New York: Routledge.

Hernández, Tanya Katerí (2002). The Buena Vista Social Club: The Racial Politics of Nostalgia. In Michelle Habell-Pallán and Mary Romero (eds.), *Latino/a Popular Culture* (pp. 61–72). New York: New York University Press.

Hesmondhalgh, David, and Melville, Caspar (2001). Urban Breakbeat Culture: Repercussions of Hip-Hop in the United Kingdom. In Tony Mitchell (ed.), *Global Noise: Rap and Hip-Hop Outside the USA* (pp. 86–110). Middletown, CT: Wesleyan University Press.

Hirst, P. and Thompson, G. (1996). *Globalisation in Question*. Cambridge, UK: Polity Press.

Howard, Keith (2002). Exploding Ballads: The Transformation of Korean Pop Music. In Timothy Craig and Richard King (eds.), *Global Goes Local: Popular Culture in Asia* (pp. 80–95). Vancouver: UBC Press.

Hu, Kelly (2005). Techno-Orientalization: The Asian VCD Experience. In John Nguyet Erni and Siew Keng Chua (eds.), *Asian Media Studies* (pp. 55–71). Malden, MA: Blackwell.

Huq, Rupa (1996). Asian Kool? Bhangra and Beyond. In Sanjay Sharma, John Hutnyk, and Ashwani Sharma (eds.), *Dis-Orienting Rhythms: The Politics of the New Asian Dance Music* (pp. 61–80). London: Zed Books.

Hutnyk, John (1996). Repetitive Beatings or Criminal Justice? In Sanjay Sharma, John Hutnyk, and Ashwani Sharma (eds.) *Dis-Orienting Rhythms: The Politics of the New Asian Dance Music* (pp. 156–89). London: Zed Books.

Hutnyk, John (2004). Magical Mystery Tourism (Debate Dub Version). In Allen Chun, Ned Rossiter, and Brian Shoesmith (eds.), *Refashioning Pop Music in Asia: Cosmopolitan Flows, Political Tempos and Aesthetic Industries* (pp. 111–26). London: Routledge Curzon.

References

Hylmo, Annika (2002). "Other" Expatriate Adolescents: A Postmodern Approach to Understanding Expatriate Adolescents among Non-US Children. In Morton G. Ender (ed.), *Military Brats and Other Global Nomads: Growing Up in Organization Families* (pp. 193–210). Westport, CT: Praeger.

Iwabuchi, Koichi (2001). *Transnational Japan.* Tokyo: Iwanami.

Iwabuchi, Koichi (2002). *Recentering Globalization: Popular Culture and Japanese Transnationalism.* Durham, NC: Duke University Press.

Iwabuchi, Koichi (2004). Introduction: Cultural Globalization and Asian Media Connections. In Koichi Iwabuchi (ed.), *Feeling Asian Modernities: Transnational Consumption of Japanese TV Dramas* (pp. 1–25). Hong Kong: Hong Kong University Press.

Iwabuchi, Koichi (2005). Discrepant Intimacy: Popular Culture Flows in East Asia. In John Nguyet Erni and Siew Keng Chua (eds.), *Asian Media Studies* (pp. 19–36). Malden, MA: Blackwell.

Jefferson, Tony (1976). Cultural Responses of the Teds: The Defense of Space and Status. In Stuart Hall and Tony Jefferson (eds.), *Resistance Through Rituals: Youth Subcultures in Post-War Britain* (pp. 81–6). Boston: Unwin Hyman.

Joseph, May (1999). *Nomadic Identities: The Performance of Citizenship.* Minneapolis: University of Minnesota Press.

Katz, Cindi (1998). Disintegrating Developments: Global Economic Restructuring and the Eroding of Ecologies of Youth. In Tracey Skelton and Gill Valentine (eds.), *Cool Places: Geographies of Youth Culture* (pp. 130–44). New York: Routledge.

Kaur, Raminder, and Kalra, Virinder S. (1996). New Paths for South Asian Identity and Musical Creativity. In Sanjay Sharma, John Hutnyk, and Ashwani Sharma (eds.), *Dis-Orienting Rhythms: The Politics of the New Asian Dance Music* (pp. 217–31). London: Zed Books.

Khiun, Liew Kai (2006). Xi Ha (Hip Hop) Zones within Global Noises: Mapping the Geographies and Cultural Politics of Chinese Hip-Hop. *Perfect Beat,* 7(4), 52–81.

Kjeldgaard, Dannie (2003). Youth Identities in the Global Cultural Economy: Central and Peripheral Consumer Culture in Denmark and Greenland. *European Journal of Cultural Studies,* 6(3), 285–304.

Kong, Lily (1996). Popular Music in Singapore: Exploring Local Cultures, Global Resources, and Regional Identities. *Environment and Planning D: Society and Space,* 14, 273–92.

Kun, Josh (2000). The Aural Border. *Theatre Journal,* 52, 1–21.

Kun, Josh (2005). *Audiotopia: Music, Race, and America.* Berkeley: University of California Press.

LaFraniere, Sharon (2006, 22 March). In the Jungle, the Unjust Jungle, a Small Victory. *New York Times*. Accessed Online, 7/10/2006.

Lai, Cherry Sze-ling and Wong, Dixon Heung Wah (2001). Japanese Comics come to Hong Kong. In Harumi Befu and Sylvie Guichard-Anguis (eds.), *Globalizing Japan: Ethnography of the Japanese Presence in Asia, Europe, and America* (pp. 111–20). New York: Routledge.

Laskewicz, Zachar (2004). Pop Music and Interculturality: The Dynamic Presence of Pop Music in Contemporary Balinese Performance. In Allen Chun, Ned Rossiter, and Brian Shoesmith (eds.), *Refashioning Pop Music in Asia: Cosmopolitan Flows, Political Tempos and Aesthetic Industries* (pp. 183–97). London: Routledge Curzon.

Lee, Keehyeung (2006). Looking Back at the Politics of Youth Culture, Space, and Everyday Life in South Korea Since the Early 1990s. Paper presented at Cultural Space and Public Sphere in Asia. Seoul, Korea. Available online at: http://asiafuture.org/csps2006/50pdf/csps2006_2b.pdf

Liebes, Tamar, and Katz, Elihu (1990). *The Export of Meaning: Cross-Cultural Readings of Dallas*. New York: Oxford University Press.

Liechty, Mark (1995). Media, Markets and Modernization: Youth Identities and the Experience of Modernity in Kathmandu, Nepal. In Vered Amit-Talai and Helena Wulff (eds.), *Youth Cultures: A Cross-Cultural Perspective* (pp. 166–201). New York: Routledge.

Liechty, Mark (2003). *Suitably Modern: Making Middle-Class Culture in a New Consumer Society*. Princeton, NJ: Princeton University Press.

Lin, Angel (2006). Independent Hip Hop Artists in Hong Kong: Cultural Capitalism, Youth Subcultural Resistance, and Alternative Modes of Cultural Production. In Shin Dong Kim and Mi Young Lee (eds.), *Mobile and Pop Culture in Asia* (pp. 45–61). Conference Proceedings. Gwangju, Korea.

Lipsitz, George (1994). *Dangerous Crossroads: Popular Music, Postmodernism and the Poetics of Place*. New York: Verso.

Lull, James (1995). *Media, Communication, Culture: A Global Approach*. New York: Columbia University Press.

Lum, Casey Man Kong (1998). The Karaoke Dilemma: On the Interaction between Collectivism and Individualism in the Karaoke Space. In Tōru Mitsui and Shūhei Hosokawa (eds.), *Karaoke Around the World: Global Technology, Local Singing* (pp. 166–77). New York: Routledge.

Lum, Casey Man Kong (2001). Karaoke and the Construction of Identity. In Alondra Nelson and Thuy Linh N. Tu with Alicia Headlam Hines (eds.), *Technicolor: Race, Technology, and Everyday Life* (pp. 121–41). New York: New York University Press.

Ma, Eric (2002a). Emotional Energy and Sub-Cultural Politics: Alternative Bands in Post-1997 Hong Kong. *Inter-Asia Cultural Studies*, 3(2), 187–200.

Ma, Eric (2002b). Translocal Spatiality. *International Journal of Cultural Studies*, 5(2), 131–52.

Mader, Roberto (1993). Globo Village: Television in Brazil. In Tony Dowmunt (ed.), *Channels of Resistance: Global Television and Local Empowerment* (pp. 67–89). London: BFI.

Maira, Sunaina Marr (2002). *Desis in the House: Indian American Youth Culture in New York City*. Philadelphia: Temple University Press.

Maira, Sunaina Marr (2004). Imperial Feelings: Youth Culture, Citizenship, and Globalization. In Marcelo M. Suárez-Orozco and Desirée Baolian Qin-Hilliard (eds.), *Globalization: Culture and Education in the New Millennium* (pp. 203–34). Berkeley: The University of California Press.

Maira, Sunaina Marr (2005). Planet Youth: Asian American Youth Cultures, Citizenship, and Globalization. In Kent Ono (ed.), *Asian American Studies After Critical Mass* (pp. 144–65). Malden, MA: Blackwell.

Maira, Sunaina Marr, and Soep, Elisabeth (eds.) (2005). *Youthscapes: The Popular, the National, the Global*. Philadelphia: University of Pennsylvania Press.

Massey, Doreen (1998). The Spatial Construction of Youth Cultures. In Tracey Skelton and Gill Valentine (eds.), *Cool Places: Geographies of Youth Cultures* (pp. 121–9). New York: Routledge.

Mayer, Vicki (2004). Please Pass the Pan: Retheorizing the Map of Panlatinidad in Communication Research. *The Communication Review*, 7(2), 113–24.

McRobbie, Angela (2000). *Feminism and Youth Culture* (2nd edn.). New York: Routledge.

McRobbie, Angela, and Garber, Jenny (1976). Girls and Subcultures: An Exploration. In Stuart Hall and Tony Jefferson (eds.), *Resistance Through Rituals: Youth Subcultures in Post-War Britain* (pp. 209–22). Boston: Unwin Hyman.

Milan, Rian (2000, 25 May). In the Jungle. *Rolling Stone*. Accessed online through Academic Search Premier, 7/12/2006.

Mitchell, Tony (ed.) (2001a). *Global Noise: Rap and Hip-Hop Outside the USA*. Middletown, CT: Wesleyan University Press.

Mitchell, Tony (2001b). Dick Lee's *Transit Lounge*: Orientalism and Pan-Asian Pop. *Perfect Beat*, 5(3), 18–45.

Mitchell, Tony (2004). Self-Orientalism, Reverse Orientalism and Pan-Asian Pop Cultural Flows in Dick Lee's *Transit Lounge*. In Koichi Iwabuchi, Stephen Muecke, and Mandy Thomas (eds.), *Rogue Flows: Trans-Asian Cultural Traffic* (pp. 95–118). Hong Kong: Hong Kong University Press.

Mitra, Ananda (1999). *Through the Western Lens: Creating National Images in Film*. Thousand Oaks, CA: Sage.

References

Morelli, Sarah (2001). "Who Is a Dancing Hero?" Rap, Hip-Hop, and Dance in Korean Popular Culture. In Tony Mitchell (ed.), *Global noise: Rap and Hip-Hop Outside the USA* (pp. 248–58). Middletown, CT: Wesleyan University Press.

Nakano, Yoshiko (2002). Who Initiates a Global Flow? Japanese Popular Culture in Asia. *Visual Communication*, 1(2), 229–53.

Nayak, Anoop (2003). *Race, Place and Globalization: Youth Cultures in a Changing World.* New York: Berg.

O'Connor, Alan (2002). Local Scenes and Dangerous Crossroads: Punk and Theories of Cultural Hybridity. *Popular Music*, 21(2), 225–36.

O'Connor, Alan (2004). Punk and Globalization: Spain and Mexico. *International Journal of Cultural Studies*, 7(2), 175–95.

Ogawa, Masashi (2001). Japanese Popular Music in Hong Kong: Analysis of Global/Local Cultural Relations. In Harumi Befu and Sylvie Guichard-Anguis (eds.), *Globalizing Japan: Ethnography of the Japanese Presence in Asia, Europe, and America* (pp. 121–30). New York: Routledge.

Ogawa, Masashi (2004). Japanese Popular Music in Hong Kong: What Does TK Present? In Allen Chun, Ned Rossiter, and Brian Shoesmith (eds.), *Refashioning Pop Music in Asia: Cosmopolitan Flows, Political Tempos, and Aesthetic Industries* (pp. 144–56). New York: Routledge-Curzon.

Ong, Aihwa (1999). *Flexible Citizenship: The Cultural Logics of Transnationality.* Durham: Duke University Press.

Ong, Aihwa (2006). Mutations in Citizenship. *Theory, Culture and Society*, 23(2–3), 499–505.

Otake, Akiko and Hosokawa, Shūhei (1998). Karaoke in East Asia: Modernization, Japanization or Asianization? In Tōru Mitsui and Shūhei Hosokawa (eds.), *Karaoke Around the World: Global Technology, Local Singing* (pp. 178–201). New York: Routledge.

Parameswaran, Radhika (2002). Local Culture in Global Media: Excavating Colonial and Material Discourses in *National Geographic. Communication Theory*, 12(3), 287–315.

Perlmutter, Tom (1993). Distress Signals: A Canadian Story – An International Lesson. In Tony Dowmunt (ed.), *Channels of Resistance: Global Television and Local Empowerment* (pp. 16–26). London: BFI.

Pidd, Helen (2007, 20 June). Fancy a Chindian? *The Guardian.* Accessed from http://lifeandhealth.guardian.co.uk/print/00,,330052494-118447,00.html on 6/19/2007.

Pilkington, Hilary, and Bliudina, Ul'iana (2002). Cultural Globalization: A Peripheral Perspective. In Hilary Pilkington, Elena Omel'chenko, Moya Flynn, Ul'iana Bliudina, and Elena Starkova (eds.), *Looking West? Cultural*

References

Globalization and Russian Youth Cultures (pp. 1–20). University Park, PA: Pennsylvania State University Press.

Pilkington, Hilary, and Johnson, Richard (2003). Peripheral Youth: Relations of Identity and Power in Global/Local Context. *European Journal of Cultural Studies*, 6(3), 259–83.

Pilkington, Hilary, and Omel'chenko, Elena (2002). Living with the West. In Hilary Pilkington, Elena Omel'chenko, Moya Flynn, Ul'iana Bliudina, and Elena Starkova (eds.), *Looking West? Cultural Globalization and Russian Youth Cultures* (pp. 201–15). University Park, PA: Pennsylvania State University Press.

Pilkington, Hilary, Omel'chenko, Elena, Flynn, Moya, Bliudina, Ul'iana, and Starkova, Elena (eds.) (2002). *Looking West? Cultural Globalization and Russian Youth Cultures*. University Park, PA: Pennsylvania State University Press.

Pollock, David C., and Van Reken, Ruth E. (1999). *The Third Culture Kid Experience: Growing Up Among Worlds*. Yarmouth, ME: Intercultural Press.

Prashad, Vijay (2000). *The Karma of Brown Folk*. Minneapolis: The University of Minnesota Press.

Prengaman, Peter (2007, 1 May). Korean Rappers Build Bridges, Define their Own Experience. *Arizona Republic*. Accessed from http://www.azcentral.com/ent/music/articles/0501Koreanrap0501.html on 5/1/2007.

Rivera, Raquel (2002). Hip Hop and New York Puerto Ricans. In Michelle Habell-Pallán and Mary Romero (eds.) *Latino/a Popular Culture* (pp. 127–43). New York: New York University Press.

Roberts, Martin (1992). "World Music" and the Global Cultural Economy. *Diaspora*, 2(2), 229–42.

Robertson, Ronald (1992). *Globalization: Social Theory and Global Culture*. Thousand Oaks, CA: Sage.

Rose, Tricia (1994). *Black Noise: Rap Music and Black Culture in Contemporary America*. Middletown, CT: Wesleyan University Press.

Russell, Mark (2003, 8 February). K-Rock, Hip-Hop Making Noise in South Korea. *Billboard*, APQ-1. Accessed via EBSCO Host on 7/30/2006.

Said, Edward W. (1979). *Orientalism*. New York: Vintage.

Sakolsky, Ron (1995). World Music at the Crossroads. In Ron Sakolsky and Fred Wei-han Ho (eds.), *Sounding Off! Music as Subversion/Resistance/Revolution* (pp. 241–5). New York: Autonomedia.

Saldanha, Arun (2002). Music, Space, Identity: Geographies of Youth Culture in Bangalore. *Cultural Studies*, 16(3), 337–50.

Sardar, Ziauddin (1999). *Orientalism*. Philadelphia: Open University Press.

Sen, Krishna and Hill, David T. (2004). Global Industry, National Politics: Popular Music in "New Order" Indonesia. In Allen Chun, Ned Rossiter, and Brian Shoesmith (eds.), *Refashioning Pop Music in Asia: Cosmopolitan Flows, Political Tempos and Aesthetic Industries* (pp. 75–88). London: Routledge Curzon.

Sharma, Sanjay (1996). Noisy Asians or "Asian Noise"?. In Sanjay Sharma, John Hutnyk, and Ashwani Sharma (eds.), *Dis-Orienting Rhythms: The Politics of the New Asian Dance Music* (pp. 32–57). London: Zed Books.

Shields, Rob (1997). Ethnography in the Crowd: The Body, Sociality and Globalization in Seoul. *Focaal: European Journal of Anthropology*. Accessed from http://http-server.carleton.ca/~rshields/focaal.html on 6/21/06.

Sinclair, John (1996). Mexico, Brazil and the Latin World. In John Sinclair, Elizabeth Jacka, and Stuart Cunningham (eds.), *New Patterns in Global Television: Peripheral Vision* (pp. 33–66). New York: Oxford University Press.

Sinclair, John, Jacka, Elizabeth, and Cunningham, Stuart (eds.) (1996). *New Patterns in Global Television: Peripheral Vision*. New York: Oxford University Press.

Singapore (2007). In *Encyclopedia Britannica*. Retrieved from Encyclopedia Britannica Online: http://search.eb.com/eb/article-9111151 on 6/21/2007.

Sklair, Leslie (1995) *Sociology of the Global System* (2nd edn.). Baltimore: Johns Hopkins University Press.

Sklair, Leslie (1999). Competing Conceptions of Globalization. *Journal of World-Systems Research*, 5(2), 143–62.

Smith, Carolyn D. (1991). *The Absentee American: Repatriate's Perspectives on America*. Bayside, NY: Aletheia Publications.

Smith, Carolyn D. (ed.) (1996). *Strangers at Home: Essays on the Effects of Living Overseas and Coming "Home" to a Strange Land*. Bayside, NY: Aletheia Publications.

Smith, Gavin J. D. (2004). Behind the Screens: Examining Constructions of Deviance and Informal Practices among CCTV Control Room Operators in the UK. *Surveillance and Society*, 2(2/3), 376–95.

Smith, Jacob (2004). "I can See Tomorrow in Your Dance": A Study of Dance, Dance Revolution and Music Video Games. *Journal of Popular Music Studies*, 16(1), 58–84.

Stapleton, Chris, and May, Chris (1990). *African Rock: The Pop Music of a Continent*. New York: Dutton.

Stone, Michael C. (2006). Garifuna Song, Groove Locale and "World Music" Mediation. In Natascha Gentz and Stefan Kramer (eds.), *Globalization, Cultural Identities, and Media Representations* (pp. 59–79). Albany: SUNY Press.

Straubhaar, Joseph (1991). Beyond Media Imperialism: Asymmetrical Interdependence and Cultural Proximity. *Critical Studies in Mass Communication*, 8(1), 39–59.

Swedenburg, Ted (2001). Islamic Hip-Hop vs. Islamophobia: Aki Nawaz, Natacha Atlas, Akhenaton. In Tony Mitchell (ed.), *Global Noise: Rap and Hip-Hop Outside the USA* (pp. 57–85). Middletown, CT: Wesleyan University Press.

Swerdlow, Joel (1999). Global Culture. *National Geographic*, August, 2–5.

Taylor, Timothy D. (1997). *Global Pop: World Music, World Markets*. New York: Routledge.

Thompson, Edward P. (1961). The Long Revolution. *New Left Review* 9, 24–33.

Tomlinson, John (1991). *Cultural Imperialism: A Critical Introduction*. Baltimore: Johns Hopkins University Press.

Tomlinson, John (1999). *Globalization and Culture*. Cambridge, UK: Polity.

Toon, Ian (2000). "Finding a Place in the Street": CCTV Surveillance and Young People's Use of Urban Public Space. In David Bell and Azzedine Haddour (eds.), *City Visions* (pp. 141–65). New York: Longman.

Valdivia, Angharad N. (2004). Latina/o Communication and Media Studies Today: An Introduction. *The Communication Review*, 7(2), 107–12.

Valentine, Gill, Skelton, Tracey, and Chambers, Deborah (1998). Cool Places: An Introduction to Youth and Youth Cultures. In Tracey Skelton and Gill Valentine (eds.), *Cool Places: Geographies of Youth Cultures* (pp. 1–32). New York: Routledge.

Verster, François (director) (2005). *A Lion's Trail* [Film]. Independent Lens. PBS.

Wald, Elijah (2001). *Narcocorrido: A Journey into the Music of Drugs, Guns, and Guerrillas*. New York: Rayo.

Waters, Malcolm (1995). *Globalization*. New York: Routledge.

Waters, Malcolm (2001). *Globalization* (2nd edn.). New York: Routledge.

Wee, C. J. W.-L. (1999). Representing the "New" Asia: Dick Lee, Pop Music, and a Singapore Modern. In Shirley Geok-Lin Lim, Larry E. Smith, and Wimal Dissanayake (eds.), *Transnational Asia Pacific: Gender, Culture, and the Public Sphere* (pp. 111–33). Urbana: University of Illinois Press.

Wilk, Richard (1995). Learning to be Local in Belize: Global Systems of Common Difference. In Daniel Miller (ed.), *Worlds Apart: Modernity Through the Prism of the Local* (pp. 110–33). New York: Routledge.

Williams, Raymond (1961). *Culture and Society 1780–1950*. Harmondsworth: Pelican Books.

Williams, Raymond (1983). *Keywords: A Vocabulary of Culture and Society* (Revised edn.). New York: Oxford University Press.

Williams, Raymond (1989). *Resources of Hope*. New York: Verso.

Williams, Raymond (1996). The Future of Cultural Studies. In John Storey (ed.), *What is Cultural Studies? A Reader* (pp. 168–77). New York: Arnold.

References

Wingett, Yvonne (2006, 8 August). Los Tigres' Ballads Capture Joy, Pain of Migrant World. *The Arizona Republic.* Accessed from AZCentral.com on 8/4/2006.

Wise, J. Macgregor (2003). Home: Territory and Identity. In J. D. Slack (ed.), *Animations (of Deleuze and Guattari)* (pp. 107–27). New York: Peter Lang.

Wise, J. Macgregor (2005). Assemblage. In Charles Stivale (ed.), *Gilles Deleuze: Key Concepts* (pp. 77–87). Chesham, UK: Acumen.

Yi, Hyangsoon (2002). [Review of *Our Nation: A Korean Punk Rock Community*]. *Journal of Asian Studies,* 61(4), 1388–9.

Young, Robert (1990). *White Mythologies: Writing History and the West.* New York: Routledge.

Zwingle, Erla (1999). Goods Move. People Move. Ideas Move. And Cultures Change. *National Geographic,* August, 12–33.

Index

a.room   105–6
ABCD   144–6
Adé, King Sunny   85
adolescence   54
Africa   14, 84–6
Afro-Caribbean   124–7, 132
Afro-Celt Sound System   79
Aguilar, Freddie   76
Ahmed, Sara   21
Ahyar, Rizal   115
All is War   133
Allende, Salvador   30
Alpert, Herb   76
alternapunk   94–6
alternative   94–6
American Chai   144
American Desi   144–5, 146
Amos, Tori   110
Anderson, Benedict   38
Anodize   103
Anokha   134
"Another Brick in the Wall
    (Part 2)"   69
anti-racism   126, 132
Aotearoa   101
Apache Indian   126–30, 146
Apartheid   80

Apgujungdong   69–71, 72, 96, 101
Appadurai, Arjun   3, 36–9, 51, 66,
    78, 87
Appiah, Kwame Anthony   150–1,
    153–4
Arawak Indians   130
Argentina   120–1, 137
Armageddon   53n
Armed Forces Radio   76
"Arranged Marriage"   128
Asian Dub Foundation (ADF)
    132, 134
Asian Kool   134
Asian Underground   134
assemblage   19–21, 23, 25
"At My Window"   89
Atlas, Natacha   128
audiotopia   77, 123–4, 131
Aurora-Maden, Sonya   135
Australia   101
authenticity   71, 85, 102, 112, 135,
    141–3
Aztlán   118

Back, Les   124–5, 127, 129–31
"Badd Indian"   130
Baja Marimba Band, The   76

168

Index

Bali 94–6, 107n
Ball and Chain 144
"Banana" 116
Banderas, Antonio 119
Barber, Benjamin 35–6
Baulch, Emma 94–6
Beethoven, Ludwig van 77
Beijing 109–11
Belize 43, 45
Bend it Like Beckham 125
Bengali 132
Bennett, Andy 92
bhangra 79, 86, 124–34, 141, 143, 147n
bhangramuffin 127
"Biko" 85
Biko, Stephen 85
"Billy Don't Be a Hero" 76
bin Laden, Osama 133
Bjork 110
Black Atlantic, The 84
Black Panthers 132
Bliudina, Ul'iana 71, 73, 78
Bollywood 39, 145
Bombay Dreams 125
border 108, 111, 121–3
Border Brujo 122
Boukman Eksperyans 90–1
Bourdieu, Pierre 10
Boym, Svetlana 19
Brazil 39
Bretton-Woods Agreement 52n
Bride and Prejudice 125
Brown, James 83
Buena Vista Social Club 79, 81–2
Burrell, Ian 126
Byrne, David 80

Cainkar, Louise 147
"Calling Out to Jah" 129
Campbell, Paul 86

Canada 35
Cantonese 109
Chávez, César 118
Chicano 118
childhood 54
Chile 30–1
Chinese 39, 48, 87, 102–4, 108–11, 113–14, 117, 137–8
Cho, Han Haejoang 68–9, 70, 107n
Chopo, El 94
Chosôn Punk 92, 96–8
Chungking Express 110
citizenship 135–40, 144
cultural 135, 137–9, 147n, 149
deep 140, 151, 154
dissenting 138–9
flexible 137
City of God 142
Clannad 79
Clapton, Eric 83
Clarke, Paul 140
Clash, The 97
Closed Circuit Television (CCTV) 59–60
club culture 143
Cocteau Twins, The 110
"Come Follow Me" 128
comic books 30–4, 40
Como, Perry 76
"Condor Pasa, El" 86
Coney Island 47
"Contrabando y Traicion" 122
Cooder, Ry 81–2
cool hunters 58
core–periphery 71–5
Cornershop 133–4
corridos 122
cosmopolitanism 150–3
Cow of OK Pasture, The 97
Cranberries, The 79, 110

169

"Crossroads" 83
Crying Nut 96–8, 107n
Cuba 81–2
Cult, The 132
cultural imperialism 32–5,
  39–42, 46, 78, 80, 83, 86–7,
  149
cultural proximity 50
culture 3–8
  mass culture 5, 8
  popular culture 8–9
  subculture 58
Curtin, Michael 110–11

Dallas 42, 46
Dance Dance Revolution (DDR)
  49
Dávila, Arlene 118–20
Davis, Susan 46–7, 52
daytimers 125, 143
De Certeau, Michel 9
deathmetal 95–6
Deleuze, Gilles 37, 129
Denmark 71–2
"Desert Rose" 86
desi 139, 141–5
Dibango, Manu 85, 87
Disney 30–4, 46, 82
DJ Jhig 101
DJ Shine 101–2
Do-It-Yourself (DIY) 92, 97,
  103–5
"Dog Tribe" 133
Dorfman, Ariel 30–4, 75, 153
Dou, Wei 110
Dr Das 134
Drug 96
Drunken Tiger 101–2, 107n
Dube, Lucky 89
Duck Rock 80
Dude, Where's the Party? 144

Dudrah, Rajinder K. 134
Duran Duran 114
Dwyer, Claire 60–2

Echobelly 135
Elvis 83
Epstein, Stephen 96–8, 107n
Erni, John 102
ethnoscape 37, 62, 87
Exile 89

Farrakhan, Louis 132
"Fe Real" 127, 130
"Feeling Begins, The" 81
Feld, Steve 81, 83
Ferrer, Ibrahim 81–2
finanscape 37, 87
Fiske, John 8–9
Forman, Murray 100
"Fragile Woman" 109
France 62
Fun^Da^Mental 132–3, 135
Fung, Anthony 110–11

Gabriel, Peter 18, 77, 79, 81, 85
Gandhi 142
Gandhi, Mahatma 128, 132, 150
Gandhi, Rajiv 128
Garofalo, Reebee 106n, 107n
Genesis 77
George, Boy 129
Gil, Gilberto 87
Gillespie, Marie 130, 147n
Gilroy, Paul 52n, 84, 152
global music 78, 89
global nomads, *see* Third Culture
  Kids
globalization 3, 27–30, 34–53, 63,
  66, 73, 75, 89, 95, 108
Globo 39
Gómez-Peña, Guillermo 122

González, Juan de Marco   81
Goodwin, Andrew   80, 83
Gore, Joe   80, 83
Graceland   77, 80–1, 85, 106n,
   107n
Green Day   94–6, 97
Greenland   71–2, 74
Griffith, Nanci   82
Guatemala   27–8
Guattari, Félix   37, 129
Guevara, Che   133

habitus   10, 39, 59, 93
Haiti   90–1
Haja Center   68–9, 96, 132
Hall, Stuart   22
Hanguk   98
Hannerz, Ulf   150–1
heavy metal   90
Hebdige, Dick   55, 58, 91, 147n
hegemony   23
Hernández, Tanya Katerí   81
hip hop   2, 17, 62, 66, 78, 90, 96,
   98–106, 120, 132–3, 143, 145,
   152–3
   in Hong Kong   102–6
   in Korea   101–2
   and Latinos   120
Hispanic   118–19
home   10, 18–19, 21–2, 25, 26–7,
   33, 38, 48, 59, 74, 138, 150
"Homeless"   85
Hong Kong   2, 39–42, 102–3,
   108–111
Hongdae   96–7
How to Read Donald Duck   30–4
Howard, Keith   98
Huntington, Samuel   24
Huq, Rupa   146
"Hush Little Baby"   86
Hustlers HC   132

"I Pray"   128, 129
"I Shot the Sheriff"   83
identity   11–15, 25n, 57, 60, 64–5,
   71–2, 90, 105, 116–17, 141,
   146, 148, 152
   antiessentialist   13
   essentialist   13, 85, 113
   strategic antiessentialism
      14–15, 90, 91, 120, 130, 143
   strategic essentialism   14, 90,
      108, 111, 116–17, 126
ideology   22–3, 113
   dominant ideology   22–3
ideoscape   37
imagined community   38
India   1, 2, 39, 53n, 76, 127–9,
   142
"India"   129
Indians   87, 112, 136, 138, 140,
   142, 145, *see also* South Asians
Indonesia   94, 107n
intermezzo culture   127
International Monetary Fund
   (IMF)   52n
Internet   92
Isidore, Sandra   83
Islam   132–3, *see also* Muslim
Italy   101
Iwabuchi, Koichi   41–2, 49–52,
   53n

Jamaica   128, 130, 147n
Japan   50–1
Japanese dramas (J-dramas)
   40–2, 50, 53n
"Jaula de Oro"   123
Jihad vs. McWorld   35–6
John, Elton   114
Johnson, Richard   83
Joi   133–4
"Jose Perez Leon"   123

Joseph, May 136
jump rope 44

Kapur, Steven *see* Apache Indian
karaoke 47–9
Karma 129
Kasson, John 47
Kathmandu 55–7, 66–8, 74
Katz, Cindi 63–4, 65–6, 67, 71,
 75, 89
Katz, Elihu 39, 42–3
Keita, Salif 85
Kidjo, Angélique 85
Kjeldgaard, Dannie 71–2
Korea 42, 44, 51, 68–71, 74–5,
 76, 96–8, 100–2, 107n
Korean Wave 42
KRS-One 62
Kula Shaker 147n
Kun, Josh 77, 124
Kuti, Fela 77, 83, 85, 87

La Haine 62, 66, 100
"La Na La" 104
"Lady" 85
Ladysmith Black Mambazo 80,
 82, 85
Last Temptation of Christ, The 81
Latino/a 119–21
Lazy Mutha Fucka (LMF) 102–6,
 110, 133
Lee, Dick 108, 111–12, 114–17,
 146
Lee, Keehyeung 75n
"Legba" 80
Legend of . . . , The 102
Lema, Ray 85
"Let's all Speak Mandarin" 115
Liebes, Tamar 39, 42–3
Liechty, Mark 55–7, 63, 66–8,
 71, 74, 75

"Life in the Lion City" 115
Linda, Solomon 82–3, 84, 85, 88
Lion King, The 82
"Lion Sleeps Tonight, The" 82
Lipsitz, George 14–15, 80–1, 83,
 88–91, 98–9, 131, 145, 151
"London Calling" 97
Looking for Bruce Lee 97
Los Angeles 52n
Lull, James 10, 16–17, 78
Lum, Casey Man Kong 48

Ma, Eric 2, 102–6
Maal, Baaba 90
Macka B 90
Mad Chinaman, The 115, 116
"Mad Chinaman, The" 116
"Magic Carpet" 128
Maira, Sunaina Marr 1, 18, 75n,
 135, 137–45, 147n, 151
Make Way for the Indian 128
"Make Way for the Indian" 130
Makeba, Miriam 76, 85
Malaysia 112
Mami, Cheb 86
Mandarin 109–10, 113, 115
Mandela, Nelson 85
Mangeshkar, Lata 128
Mardi Gras Indians 15, 90
Marley, Bob 83
Massey, Doreen 27, 59, 74
Mattelart, Armand 30–4, 75, 153
Matthews, Dave 79
Mayer, Vicki 120–1
"Mbube" 82, 84, 86, 88
McLaren, Malcolm 18, 80, 92
McRobbie, Angela 58
mediascape 37, 66, 87
Metallica 94
Mexico 92–4, 121–3
Mickie Eyes 101

Milan, Rian 82–3, 86
Million Dollar Baby 151
Mitchell, Joni 114
Mitchell, Tony 100–1, 111,
   114–15
"Modern Asia" 116
modernity 42, 49–51, 66, 111,
   113–14, 116
mods 58, 59
Monsoon Wedding 125
moral panic 58
"Movie Over India" 127
MTV 106
Mumbai 53n
Muslim 60–2, 137–9, *see also*
   Islam
"Myungdong Calling" 97

Nakano, Yoshiko 40–2
narcocorridos 122
Nation of Islam 132
National Geographic 29–30, 33,
   34, 38, 45, 53n
Native Americans 15, 90, 130–1
Nawaz, Aki 132, 133
Nayak, Anoop 64–5, 66, 75
N'Dour, Youssou 77, 85, 87
Neville Brothers 15
New Asian 114–16
New York City 64, 66, 67, 142–3
Newcastle 64–5
Night to Night 89
Nirvana 96, 97
No Reservations 127, 130
Nomad 89
"Non, Je Ne Regrette Rien" 63
norteño 122
nostalgia 142–3

"Obatala" 80
occidentalism 24

O'Connor, Alan 93–4
Ogawa, Masashi 40–1
Omel'chenko, Elena 73
Ong, Aihwa 137, 138
Orange Tribe 69–71, 75
orientalism 23–4, 25n, 116, 131,
   142
   self-orientalism 24, 114, 116
Oryema, Geoffrey 85, 87, 89
*Our Nation: A Korean Punk Rock
   Community* 107n
Our Nation, Volume One 96, 98
Outkaste 134
"Over the Rainbow" 97

"Pacas de Kilo" 122
Pandya, Piyush Dinker 144
panlatinidad 108, 117–24
Passage to India 142
Passion 81
Passion Sources 81
"Pata Pata" 85
Patel, Krutin 145
Paul, Frankie 128
People's Action Party (PAP)
   112–13, 115
People's Republic of China (PRC)
   40–1, 48, 102–3, 109, 111,
   113, 117
Philippines 76
Phiri, Ray 85
Piaf, Edith 63, 79
Pilkington, Hilary 71–4, 78
Pink Floyd 69
Pinochet, Auguste 30–1
Plus From Us 81
power 16–18, 27
   cultural power 17–18
Prashad, Vijay 138, 141–2
Priest, Maxi 127, 128
"Prisoner" 89

Punjabi 125–7, 132
punk 58, 78, 90, 91–8, 114, 123, 133
  in Bali 94–6
  in Barcelona 94
  in Britain 92
  in Korea 92, 96–8
  in Mexico City 92, 93–4
  in New York 92
Puno, Rico J. 76

Qawwali 133

raags 128
Raffles, Sir Stamford 115
rai 86
Rand, Ayn 77
"Rasa Sayang" 115
Rastafarianism 129
Real World Records 77, 81
reggae 95–6, 124–30, 147n
"Religion" 129
REM 82
Remain in Light 83
rhizome 129, 148
Rivera, Raquel 120
Roach, Max 99
Roberts, Martin 87–8
Robertson, Ronald 29
rock music 74
Rolling Stones 79, 83
Rose, Tricia 100
Rush 77
Russia 72–4

Said, Edward 25n
Saldanha, Arun 2
Sardar, Ziauddin 24
"Sardinia Memories (After Hours)"
  89
Seeger, Pete 82
"Semi-Charmed Life" 69

Senegal 85, 90
Seo Taiji and the Boys 96, 98
Sex Pistols, The 92
Shakira 86
Shambala, Joseph 86
Shankar, Ravi 128
Sharma, Sanjay 132–3
Shields, Rob 70–1
Shin, Hae Chul 69
Simon, Paul 18, 77, 79, 80, 82,
  83, 85–6, 106n
Sinatra, Frank 76
Singapore 111–15
Singh, Malkit 128
Singh, Talvin 134
So 77
"Somos Mas Americanos" 123
son 81–2
Sonic Youth 94
soul 125
"Soul Makossa" 85
"Sound of Da Police" 62
sound systems 124–7, 143, 147n
South Africa 80–1, 83, 89, 91,
  106n
South Asians 109, 124–36,
  137–46, *see also* Indians
Spain 94, 101
Sting 79, 86
structures of common difference
  44–5, 113, 117
Sudan 63–4, 65
Sumo wrestling 44–5
Supercat, Wild Apache 130
Supermarket 107n
surveillance 57–61, 143
Swank, Hilary 151
Swedenburg, Ted 132

Taiwan 41–2, 50
Talking Heads, The 83

Tangherlini, Timothy   107n
Tanzania   136
Taxi Driver   62, 66
Taylor, Timothy   81, 85, 128
technoscape   37, 87
Teds   58, 59, 66
teenagers   55–7
Teens   55–6
television   53n, 72
territory   10–13, 15–16, 18, 20,
    48–9, 59, 61–2, 77–8, 93,
    105–6, 108, 131, 140–3, 146,
    148, 150
  cultural territorialization   49,
    106, 108, 146, 148, 150
  deterritorialization   15–16, 152
  reterritorialization   16, 78, 131,
    134–5, 144, 152
theme parks   46–7
Third Culture Kids (TCKs)
    19–22
Third Eye Blind   69
Thompson, E. P.   7
Thompson, John B.   16
Tiger JK   101
Tigres Del Norte, Los   122–3,
    137
Time for Change   129
Tjader, Cal   76
Tokens, The   82
Toon, Ian   60
Transglobal Underground   128
"Tumba del Mojado, La"   123

U2   79
"Uknuwudafuckimsayin"   104
Umali, Rosco   101
Uniendo Fronteras   123
United States   121–2, 140
Us   81
Utama, Sang Nila   115

Valdez, Basil   76
Video Compact Disk (VCD)   40,
    53n
"Vivan Los Mojados"   123
Voodoo Queens, The   133–5

Wakafrika   85
Wald, Elijah   122–3
Warner Music   106
Washington Consensus   52n
Waters, Malcolm   37, 53n
We Are Three   134
Weavers, The   86
Wee, C. J. W.-L.   116
Wemba, Papa   77, 85
Wild East   128, 130
Wild Tchoupitoulas   15
Wilk, Richard   43–6, 78, 87, 113,
    118
Williams, Andy   76
Williams, Raymond   4–7
"Wimoweh"   82, 85, 86
Wong, Faye   108, 109–11, 117,
    146
Wong, Kar-Wai   110
"WORD"   101
World Bank   52n
world music   76, 79
World of Music, Arts, and Dance
    (WOMAD)   81

"Yelle"   90
"You are Happy, I am Happy"
    110
Young, Neil   114
youth   54–75, 137–143, 149–50
youthscape   62, 75n

Zap Mama   79
Zwingle, Erla   29–30, 34
Zydeco   79

CPSIA information can be obtained
at www.ICGtesting.com
Printed in the USA
JSHW042305261122
33647JS00006B/23